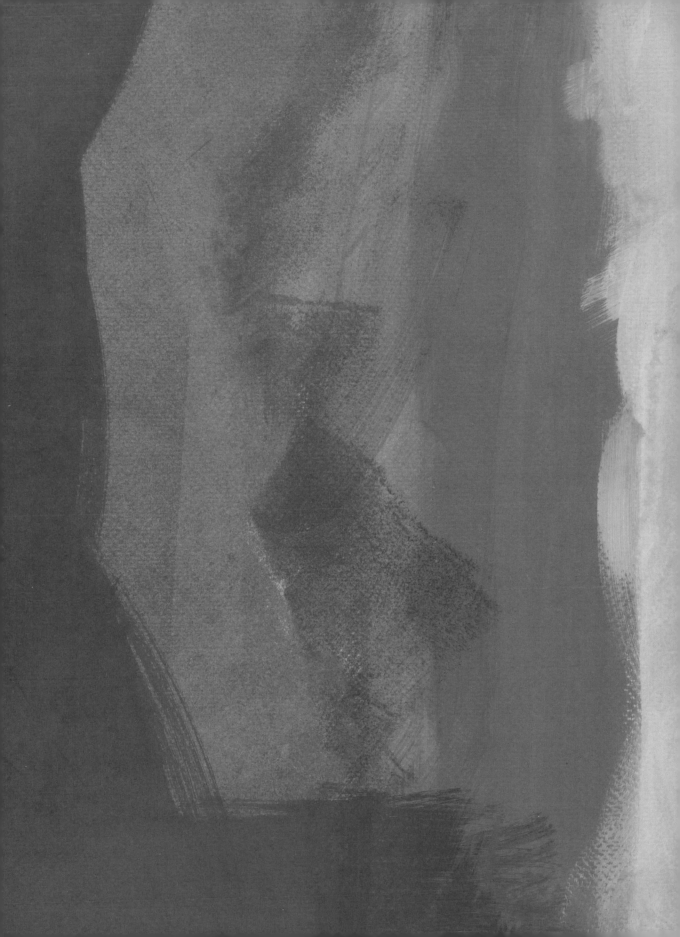

THALI

THALI

Maunika Gowardhan

Hardie Grant

BOOKS

CONTENTS

INTRODUCTION

A REGIONAL CELEBRATION

Thalis are a celebration of fresh ingredients that encompass the whole range of flavours of Indian cuisine and display, to perfection, its sheer regional variety. In homes right across the subcontinent, the produce grown and cooked locally is reflected by what is served on each platter.

'Thali' literally translates as 'a large plate'; it has come to mean a complete meal on a platter, made up of a variety of components including curries, stir-fries and dry vegetable dishes, all served in little steel bowls, historically known as *dunas*. In ancient India, thalis were served on disposable plates made of dried banyan tree leaves. Even today, regional thalis can be served on leaves at weddings or *pujas* (a religious event) as a way of marking the occasion.

When it comes to understanding the cuisine of India, there really is no better way than to explore a thali. Hot, sour, spicy, crispy, tangy and sweet: these are the flavours our palates yearn for, and the thali offers the marriage of all these flavours. With a myriad of vibrant colours and diversity, there are regional varieties within each community, each one not only full of flavour, but offering an insight into the local spices and ingredients of each place. The techniques of cooking vary too – including steaming, preserving, deep-frying, slow-cooking, baking and smoking – a huge variety comes into play in just one meal.

Historically, planning and organising a thali has also focused heavily on its nutritional value, aiming to strike a balance of nutritional qualities as well as flavours. Over time, however, the celebratory platters have sometimes become too rich, ladened with heavy food, and served without enough time for this fast-paced generation to sample all the dishes in one sitting.

As a result, age-old recipes have become less prominent in thalis, and are in danger of being lost or forgotten altogether. Thalis are such a wonderful tradition, and an element of Indian dining that will stand the test of time if we celebrate them for their geographical context, regional recipes, local flavours and spices. This is something we now see happening in cities across the Indian subcontinent, where thalis are served as an eat-all-you-can feast, with a reasonable price point – it's no wonder they are hugely popular.

WHAT MAKES
A GREAT THALI?

Including grains, pulses, protein and dairy, and even fresh fruit or dessert, a thali feels like a complete experience for the palate. Indian cuisine thrives on produce grown locally, and each region is rich in recipes concocted from a variety of vegetables including aubergines (eggplants), cauliflower, leafy green vegetables, jackfruit and green beans, to name just a few. Rich in vitamins and minerals, a lot of these make up the curries, stir-fries and snacks included in a thali, alongside wholemeal breads that are used as a means to scoop up the curries.

When it comes to spices, their warmth and flavour add another dimension to all the fresh ingredients. Ginger, garlic, cumin, chilli, black pepper, fennel, cloves and fenugreek are just some of them. Pickles, chutneys and spiced powders are served in smaller quantities as they pack a punch of heat and spice, so a little goes a long way. They also help to balance the meal – a spicy curry with a sweet chutney or pickle, and vice versa – bringing it all together.

Crispy fried pakoras and fritters have always been an essential part of a thali. They give the meal texture, and are a great way to showcase seasonal vegetables and use up leftovers.

A sweet dish is also a must. Some communities in the north of India believe that the inclusion of more sweets within a thali is a sign of prosperity, abundance and flamboyance.

As much as accompaniments might seem like an afterthought, one of my favourite things to have along with a thali when I was younger was a big glass of chilled *chaas*: buttermilk blended with cumin, ginger and fresh coriander (cilantro). Not only is this a cooling drink great in warmer weather, but it also aids digestion after a meal, helping your body break down all the food.

MY THALI EXPERIENCE

My family hails from the west of India, from Mumbai in the state of Maharashtra and, being a Mumbaikar, thalis have always been a part of every occasion and meal we have eaten, from the simplest basic thali at home to meals ladened with comfort food for *pujas*, special occasions, or Sunday lunches. We enjoyed the ultimate thali to mark the celebration after my traditional Indian wedding, where over 20 dishes were served to 1,500 guests in silver thalis and bowls.

On my travels to Kerala, on the coast of south-western India, savouring a *sadya* has been a feast for the eyes and belly. A *sadya* is a banquet which is traditionally served during the festival of Onam or at family gatherings. It is a vegetarian thali brimming with a variety of local vegetables, pulses and leafy greens. Most *sadyas* can include between 40 and 50 dishes, which are served in the traditional way on banana leaves. Diners are seated on the floor for the meal, which includes some of south India's foremost delicacies.

I reminisce, too, over a particular balmy Sunday afternoon strolling through Colaba, in Mumbai, on my way to sample something truly spectacular: the delights of a Bohri *thaal*. The people of the Bohri community, who originally migrated from Yemen to Gujarat, are renowned for their unique cooking style, with dishes including delectable meat curries and biryanis. Bohri *thaals* are essentially large platters on which the food is served. Six or eight people gather around the *thaal*, sharing food and stories, and coming together with family and friends. Meals are served over several courses and begin with *mithas* (sweets), as it is considered auspicious, followed by *kharaas* (savoury dishes). The meal ends with another sweet. Communal eating has been a part of Indian households for centuries, and Bohri meals are just one such representation of people getting together to savour flavours synonymous with local cities.

Growing up in India, eating a thali was when I felt most at home: surrounded by family, feasting with ladlefuls of curries served across the dinner table as we shared conversations about our days, our lives, books, politics and food. Second and third servings were always welcome, and meals were savoured.

BUILD YOUR OWN THALI

As anyone who has been confronted with a thali for the first time knows, the variety of dishes can seem a little overwhelming. As you go through the meal, however, you realise that each element in the thali lends something unique to the overall experience in terms of taste and texture. A thali is essentially a complete meal served on a single plate, and one that is a taste sensation with each successive bite.

So, what does a complete meal like this include? A thali should offer:

+ A stir-fried, dry vegetable dish.

+ A crispy fried snack, like pakoras or fritters, *vadas* or a savoury snack.

+ A soupy dal.

+ Meat, fish, vegetables, pulses or beans, cooked in a gravy-based curry.

+ Wholemeal breads, generally unleavened, to scoop up the curries, followed by a portion of rice.

+ Pickles and chutneys, to introduce a dimension of warmth and sweetness.

+ No thali (or for that matter any Indian meal!) would be complete without a sweet dish, dessert or even a simple fresh fruit.

Accompaniments like a fresh salad, raita or plain yoghurt and *papad* also lend balance and give a cooling effect, as well as a change of texture between each bite of food.

There are plenty of recipes in each of these chapters in this book, alongside advice on how to balance the variety of flavours and textures.

HOW TO EAT YOUR THALI

The various dishes that make up the thali are arranged on the platter so that you enjoy them in a particular order, but the order in which you begin the thali (left to right or right to left), or even which course is eaten first, can vary between regions. Some regions are known to begin their meal with a sweet dish, as they do in Gujarat, while in Bengali thalis, for instance, the meal begins with *shukto*, a vegetable curry made with bitter gourd. The idea is that beginning the meal with something bitter will open our palates, and also aid digestion throughout the meal.

Thalis are traditionally eaten with your hand. When I think about how I grew up eating food at home, I honestly cannot imagine tucking into a plate of rice topped with steaming dal and ghee in any other way than with my fingers: mixing the rice and dal really well so there was more than enough rice to soak up all that flavoursome, soupy dal. Eating with my fingers makes me savour every bite – my fingertips take the time to gather the right amount food before the next mouthful while I chew the last – and sparks that true feeling of home comfort within me.

Even today, while serving my family a bowl of fish curry and rice, I am probably the only one at the table using my hand rather than traditional cutlery. Every bite of coconut and spice-ladened gravy, rice and a crispy fried piece of fish is sublime, as I mix it all before taking a mouthful. It's an emotional connection and one through which I feel closer to the food I cook and eat. It feels good for many reasons – more than I can explain.

So when you make your thali, try eating with your hands (and keep a spoon on the side, just in case you need one!). Using your fingers, break a piece of chapatti, fold it over and scoop up the curry with it, followed by a bite of crispy pakora and a little sweet pickle. That is ultimate thali joy!

HOW TO USE THIS BOOK

I am a self-taught cook, and over the years, amidst all the little triumphs I've had in my kitchen in a quest for the perfect curry, I've also made my fair share of mistakes. I didn't have a rule book to tell me how I should cook. I landed on my feet after years of practice and a few staple spices that have always steered me on the right track. With some key spices in hand, you can make anything taste good. I hope that when you start using this book, you will see that these spices contribute to dishes that are uncomplicated and fuss-free, but most of all, full of flavour.

With this book, I have aimed to celebrate thalis, giving you both popular regional recipes as well as lesser-known dishes that I am sure you will enjoy, creating them with ingredients that are commonly available in most supermarkets. The recipes are accessible and a reflection of how, with just a few dishes, you can create something truly special that Indians have been enjoying for centuries. *Thali* is a celebration of communities that have shared their dinner tables with me throughout my travels over the last decade, and have been kind enough to share their recipes with me: recipes that have been part of their families for generations, and have now become staples in my home, too.

I have divided the book into seven chapters: stir-fried vegetables, snacks, dal, curries made with chicken, lamb, seafood and vegetables, breads, condiments and finally desserts. I feel each of these elements individually brings something unique, and they become complete when you put them together on one plate.

Each recipe in this book is versatile enough to serve as part of a thali or enjoyed on its own. I almost always find myself staring blankly into the fridge an hour before dinner, wondering what to make. Using this book for everyday cooking, I can choose just a couple of dishes from different sections to make a meal: perhaps a simple chicken curry served with chapattis and raita.

Alternatively, you can choose dishes from many more sections, turning your meal into a thali-inspired feast for family or friends. When I cook a thali at home, I pick and choose from the many elements in this book. Design your thali based on time, ingredients and the occasion you plan on cooking for. Keeping in mind the rule of balance in your meal, you can play around with curries, snacks and accompaniments. There is no limit to how many bowls you can serve: for me a simple thali including a plain dal, vegetable curry, chapattis, rice, plain yoghurt and pickle is as delicious as an ostentatious one including seven or eight curries. Each recipe in the book serves four as a main meal, so there is plenty to go around when you are assembling the thali.

At the back of this book on pages 209–214, I have also shared some regional combinations so you can see which recipes come from communities across Gujarat, Andhra Pradesh, Bengal and Punjab. Plus there are some menu plans on page 217, brimming with ideas for a vegan thali, vegetarian thali or fish thali, with suggestions for which accompaniments, snacks and pickles can be served with each curry.

After nearly two decades of professional cooking, my advice to anyone cooking from this book and following my recipes is to use them as your guide. Let them lead the way for you until you find your feet and develop the confidence to add and take away ingredients as you see fit, making the recipe your own: using an instinct and sensibility that we all yearn for when we are adding spices to the pan, stirring up a homemade curry and assembling a delectable thali from scratch.

I hope the aromas of these recipes remind you of home and bring you comfort – as they do me – and take you on a journey through food, helping you delve just a little more into what I experienced on my travels across India. Bringing a slice of that to your dinner tables will make me beyond happy!

KITCHEN ESSENTIALS

SPICES

Spices are an integral part of Indian culture and identity. A spice cupboard always holds pride of place in our kitchens. Each spice can make all the difference to a well-balanced and flavoured dish. Indian cooking uses spices in a way unlike any other cuisine across the world. Some are roasted before they are used, then pounded into a coarse mix or finely ground, while others are tempered whole in hot oil.

Across all the regional cuisines, spices are used for flavour, colour and health benefits. Some spices also work as preservatives in pickles and curries. Flavour is imparted as the spices are heated, crushed or pounded. When you crush spices in a stone grinder, they release their oils, which also happens when they are added to hot oil. Generally, whole spices are added at the beginning of cooking, while ground spices are added halfway through or at the end of the cooking process. The longer the spice is simmering in your curry, the more warmth, depth and flavour it yields.

Keeping in mind that food is also a feast for the eyes, the look of the final dish is equally important when cooking Indian food. Colour and texture are crucial, and spices are responsible for imparting much of this to the dish. A vibrant chilli powder can do wonders for the colour of a curry, while turmeric gives that golden yellow hue. One of the most underrated ways of using spices is to have them coarsely ground, but I use them in this way in many recipes. The flavour of coarsely crushed spices differs vastly to when they are finely ground or whole. My *Rajasthani Khade Masale Ka Murgh* recipe (page 62) is the ideal recipe that mixes coarse spices with caramelised fried onions and chicken to bring them to life.

For anyone beginning their journey into Indian cooking, I want to share the top tips that have served me well through the years:

- ✦ Add spices sparingly, as you would salt or pepper; they are there to bring warmth, depth and earthy tones to the dishes you cook, while lending desired heat.

- ✦ Remember you can always add more, but you can't take away.

- ✦ Storing spices away from sunlight ensures they stay fresh and last longer.

- ✦ Before you begin cooking, make sure you have all your ingredients to hand. With hot oil, it is easier to add spices when you have everything near you, and it will also prevent spices from burning in the pan.

It is imperative to check you have fresh spices for the recipes you cook. If spices have been on your kitchen shelf for years, the chances are they aren't doing justice to the curries you are cooking. Buying your spices in smaller quantities means you will always have fresher stock.

MY TOP FIVE SPICES

My top five are a staple in my spice tin, and they're the ones I always recommend everyone to stock up on. With these as your base, you can make any recipe. Even if the recipe seems to have a long list of ingredients, just a quick read through will reassure you that you already have most of them! This is a good starting point, and you can always build up your stock of spices, adding more as you go along.

1. Cardamom/*Elaichi*
One of the most expensive spices in the world, these green pods grow widely across the Malabar Coast, which is where the Arab traders landed. They brought it with them to Egypt, Greece and the Middle East. Green cardamom flourishes on the hillsides with plenty of rainfall and is picked just before ripening so the pods don't split. It is then sun-dried.

Appearing in masala chai, curries, biryanis and most Indian sweets, there is no doubt this is a much-loved spice in Indian cooking, prized for its subtle flavour. Use green cardamom whole with the skin on and, once the dish is ready, you can discard the pods. If a recipe requires just the seeds, grind them in a pestle and mortar or spice grinder, which will impart loads more flavour. When making masala chai I usually roughly bash the green cardamom (skin and seeds) in a pestle and mortar before adding to the chai and letting it simmer gently. If you are using just the seeds, add the green outer skin to your sugar jar for a mild floral aroma.

Black cardamom, the larger cousin, has a wonderful, smoky flavour and depth, so must be used sparingly in savoury dishes.

2. Chilli Powder/*Mirchi*
Chilli powder is used for heat but also the colour it imparts to dishes. Chillies are such an integral part of Indian cooking, it is hard to believe there was a time when they didn't exist in India at all! Vasco Da Gama's arrival in Goa (1498 BCE) was the start of chilli cultivation in the region, as they thrived in the climate and soil. Slowly, over many years, chillies made their way to the west and north of the country.

Now there are over 200 varieties grown in India!

As well as whole chillies and ground chillies, my favoured chilli has always been Kashmiri chilli, partly because it is so readily available around the world, but also because of how well it works in Indian recipes. Kashmiri chillies are a bright red variety with a moderate heat (which means you can get away with adding more if you like your dishes spicy). Kashmiri chilli powder has a smoky taste and vibrant red hue that is ideal for curries where you are looking for heat, flavour and colour. This is the one powdered spice I always insist people try to get hold of.

If you're not able to get hold of Kashmiri chilli powder, I always advise opting for a mild (unsmoked) paprika, which will give the desired colour, then adding a pinch of cayenne pepper for the required heat. You can also use a commercially available chilli powder, which is sold as hot, medium or mild and is usually a blend.

Whole dried chillies soaked in warm water make the perfect chilli paste to use in curries as well as pickles. Byadagi chillies, grown in Karnataka, are deep rich and red in colour, with a minimal heat.

In terms of the fresh variety, I always opt for green birds-eye chillies, which lend a lovely heat to curries, or can be pickled whole or used in a green chilli relish (see *Maharashtrian Thecha* on page 186).

3. Coriander/Dhania
Coriander's mild citrus and floral flavour resonates through a curry when added in powdered form, which can been hugely

different to the flavour imparted by the coarsely crushed seeds. This is one of the oldest spices and has been around for over 3,000 years. Sold in large sacks at wholesale markets across India, including in Old Delhi, it's hard to walk past the by-lanes without getting a whiff of the spice. I buy the seeds and then grind them in batches, which last a few weeks. Meaning I always have freshly ground coriander to use in my dishes. Adding ground coriander lends a mellow flavour to a dish while toning down the flavours of other spices.

Coriander (cilantro) leaves are my favourite herb and used commonly as a garnish. My family recipe for fish curry uses coriander leaves as well as the stems and root, which makes an aromatic base and lends a wonderful flavour, so make sure to use the fresh coriander stems, too. In my thali recipes, I have used them in *Kothimbir Vade* (page 150), which is so moreish.

4. Cumin/*Jeera*
If, like me, you grew up in India, you would remember the *jeera golis*, a sweet tangy candy made with ground cumin, dried mango and sugar. It was available at my local grocer's in Mumbai for just a few *paise*. The joy of eating these little treats was immense.

Cumin is an ancient seed used since the Vedic times. It has many health properties and is usually prescribed in Ayurveda, as it aids digestion.

Cumin grows best in soil that is not rich. The fewer nutrients in the soil, the richer the flavour of the spice, so it's no surprise that Rajasthan produces some of the most intensely flavoured cumin.

The seeds are light brown and have a distinctive aroma – peppery and warm. Available whole or powdered, I always stock up on the seeds and then grind them coarsely or finely depending on what I need them for. From *chaat*, curries and raita to drinks and kebabs, a pinch of coarsely crushed *jeera* is a game changer.

Cumin is also ground with coriander seeds, a mixture commonly known as *dhania-jeera* (see page 20), one of the most essential blends in Indian cooking. You will also find other varieties of cumin, including *kala jeera* and *shahi jeera*.

5. Turmeric/*Haldi*
Renowned the world over both for its culinary uses and medicinal properties, this versatile spice is the soul of Indian cooking. Native to south India, it thrives in hot summers and in good-quality soil, although it is now widely grown in many countries across Asia. Fresh turmeric resembles ginger and is bright orange on the inside. The vibrant colour, which comes from the presence of the pigment curcumin, enriches regional dishes. Turmeric root is widely used in pickles (you'll find my favourites in this collection) and curries. Grating some fresh turmeric while cooking my spicy scrambled eggs for breakfast is the best start to my day. The ground variety is widely used in curries, baking and drinks.

OTHER SPICES FOR YOUR STORECUPBOARD

You will also find these spices in many of my recipes, so you may want to expand your stock of spices.

Asafoetida/*Hing*
A pungent spice derived from the fennel plant, the pungency reduces as it cooks. It works perfectly in dals, stir-fried vegetable dishes and even pickles. Asafoetida aids digestion and mimics the flavour of garlic, so it is often used in place of garlic in certain vegetarian recipes (in religions such as Jainism, the use of garlic is avoided). Use it in small quantities, adding the spice to hot oil to release its flavour. Asafoetida comes in a variety of grades and strengths, as well as in different colours, as I have found on my travels to the spice market in Old Delhi. The classic dish *Hingwalli Dal* uses the extra-strong variety.

Cassia Bark/*Dalchini*
This has got to be one of my favourite spices. Cassia bark is the thick outer bark of the cinnamon tree. It is much darker than cinnamon, with a rich flavour, sweetness and an undertone of heat. It works brilliantly with lamb and in a variety of meat curries. The warm, sweet notes of this mild spice make it common in ground spice blends and pastes.

The cinnamon that is widely available as powder or sticks is a variety of true cinnamon. It is the inner bark of the cinnamon tree, light brown in colour, a strip of bark that curls inwards with a thin crumbly texture. Some of the best cinnamon I have cooked with was when a friend gifted me some from her home town in Sri Lanka.

I tend to add cassia bark to most of my recipes rather than cinnamon, although you can swap one for the other. I think cassia lends something truly special, so if you can, do try and get hold of some. It is available in Asian grocer's and larger supermarkets.

Carom Seeds/*Ajwain*
Carom seeds are commonly used in snacks, street food, vegetable dishes and Indian breads. With a slightly pungent flavour similar to oregano, the seeds are small and light brown in colour. Because of how strong this spice is, a little goes a long way. Adding *ajwain* when tempering spices to cook dal is wonderful. My favourite recipe using this spice is the *Ajwain Parathas* (page 168).

Dried Mango Powder/*Amchur*
Made from raw, green mangoes, *amchur* is beige in colour and lends a citrus tang to dishes, especially in recipes that require a fruity, sour flavour without the moisture. It is perfect added to barbecues, tikkas, grilled meats and seafood, or even to stuffed parathas. It is available in all Asian supermarkets and also online.

Fenugreek/*Methi*
Fenugreek, or *methi* as it is known in Indian cooking, has a savoury and slightly bitter flavour. This can be found fresh at Asian grocer's, in seed form, or as dried leaves. The dried leaves, also known as *kasoori methi*, are perfect for finishing a curry and complement other spices really well in many dishes.

Pomegranate Powder/*Anardana*
Widely used in north Indian cooking, pomegranate powder has a coarse texture and is used for its tangy/tart flavour in curries and chutneys. It is made by grinding dried pomegranate seeds and works really well in stir-fried or meat dishes. It is used in a variety of ways, including, fresh seeds, molasses and juice. This powder version adds fruitiness to a dish while also thickening curries and lending texture.

SPICE BLENDS

GARAM MASALA
Hot Spice Mix

MAKES ABOUT 50 G (2 OZ)

8 cm (3¼ in) piece of cassia bark or
  cinnamon stick
3 heaped tbsp coriander seeds
2 tbsp green cardamom pods, seeds only
½ tbsp cloves
1 tbsp black peppercorns
4 black cardamom pods, seeds only

Heat a frying pan (skillet) over a low heat.
Add all the spices to the hot pan and dry-
fry for 6–7 minutes, shaking the pan, until
toasted and fragrant. Be careful not to burn
the spices. Turn off the heat and leave to
cool. Transfer to a blender or coffee grinder
then grind to create a fine powder. Store in
a clean, airtight jar.

DHANIA-JEERA
Coriander & cumin powder

MAKES ABOUT 50 G (2 OZ)

6 tbsp coriander seeds
2 tbsp cumin seeds
2 dried mild red Kashmiri chillies
2 dried bay leaves

Heat a frying pan (skillet) over a low heat.
Add the coriander seeds, cumin seeds
and chillies to the hot pan and dry-fry for
2–3 minutes, stirring well until toasted and
fragrant. Be careful not to burn the spices.
Turn off the heat and leave to cool. Transfer
to a blender or coffee grinder with the bay
leaves and grind to create a fine powder.
Store in a clean, airtight jar.

PANCH PHORON
Bengali five-spice mix

MAKES ABOUT 50 G (2 OZ)

1 tbsp black mustard seeds
1 tbsp fennel seeds
1 tbsp nigella seeds
1 tbsp cumin seeds
1 tbsp fenugreek seeds

Combine all the seeds and store in a clean,
airtight jar.

FRESH & STORECUPBOARD INGREDIENTS

Plenty of the large supermarkets these days stock all the spices and ingredients to make cooking curries seamless. You can also find many of these spices and fresh ingredients online (check out Spices of India, Red Rickshaw or even Amazon). If you have an Asian grocer's nearer to where you live, that's like a treasure trove of Indian ingredients, and you'll find everything you need for the recipes in this book.

Chapatti Flour/*Atta*
Stoneground wholemeal (whole wheat) flour with a grainy texture is used for many Indian breads, including chapatti, layered parathas and puris (see Breads & Rice, pages 164–168).

Chickpea or Gram Flour/*Besan*
A pale yellow, gluten-free, finely ground flour made from chickpeas (garbanzos), this is used for curries, fried snacks and breads. It is also used as a thickening agent.

Coconut
Many of the recipes in this book use grated coconut, especially the recipes from coastal regions. It can be found in Asian grocer's, where it is usually sold as a frozen. I normally buy a few packets and use them for chutneys, curries and stir-fries. If you cannot get hold of frozen grated or fresh coconut, you can opt for desiccated coconut. A good tip is to soak the desiccated coconut in hot water for 15–20 minutes before use, then drain and use to make your coconut paste or chutney. Soaking helps add the moisture required to allow you to grind it to a smooth paste.

Curry Leaves/*Karipatta*
There are lots of online stores now delivering fresh curry leaves to your doorstep. Again, you can find these at Asian grocer's, where they are sold in large bags. They freeze well, too. You can opt for the dried variety if you prefer: just make sure to crush them and add at the end of cooking.

Dal
Even small supermarkets, and certainly major ones and Asian stores, will stock a range of pulses for your cooking. All the types used in this book should be easy to find. I mainly use chana dal, moong dal and toor dal.

CHANA DAL A dried split pulse that is used commonly in Indian cooking. As a dal, it holds its shape and yields a creamy consistency when cooked.

MOONG DAL Also known as mung beans, these are small round green lentils that are used whole, husked or halved. When husked and halved they are yellow in colour. They are readily available in stores and online. It cooks very quickly and is easy to digest.

TOOR DAL One of the most commonly used lentils in south Asian recipes, toor dal lends a creamy consistency and is great for cooking *Goan Dalicha Ras* (page 140) or a classic *Andhra Tomato Paappu* (page 142).

Fresh Green Chillies
The heat of green chillies resides within the membrane and lends a unique flavour to Indian food. Slitting chillies lengthways keeps the seeds intact while still adding a bit of heat. Bird's-eye green chillies are available at Asian grocer's and major supermarkets.

Ginger/*Adrak*
Pale yellow, fresh ginger root can be sliced, grated and chopped for a savoury pungent flavour. Peel off the skin before use.

Ghee

Clarified butter is commonly used in Indian cooking. It has a high smoking point and a wonderful nutty flavour that is perfect for frying and simmering curries.

Jaggery

Unrefined Indian cane sugar, jaggery, is deliciously rich in flavour. It's perfect for sweetening curries and also great in desserts, although you can swap it for soft brown sugar.

Oil

For everyday recipes, I always opt for vegetable oil or sunflower oil. Both are flavourless and colourless, which means the spices render their flavour to the oil.

For pickles and some curries, I use mustard oil, which has a distinct, pungent flavour, for its preservative properties. It is widely used in the east of India. Mustard oil is readily available in major supermarkets and Asian stores. Mustard oil is often labelled 'For External Use Only', which usually causes questions and confusion due to the high levels of erucic acid in mustard oil, although Indians have been cooking with and consuming it for centuries, and it is also known to be used in some Italian recipes.

Potatoes

Rooster potatoes work best in curries because they hold better in a gravy – you don't want the potatoes to get too mushy.

Rice

There are so many ways to cook rice and it's the thing I get always get asked about. This is my foolproof method, which has served me well for years and gives you fluffy, separated grains. Using basmati rice lends a gorgeous light texture and wonderful aroma.

150 g (5 oz/¾ cup) basmati rice
300 ml (10 fl oz/1¼ cups) water
salt, to taste

Wash the rice in cold running water twice; this will rid the rice of starch. Bring the water to the boil in a small saucepan. Add the washed rice, along with the salt. Stir and, as it starts to boil, reduce the heat to a simmer, cover the saucepan and cook for 10 minutes. Turn off the heat and let it rest for 5 minutes until all the water has been absorbed. Use a fork to fluff up the rice, and serve warm.

Tamarind

The tart, tangy fruit of the tamarind tree is a commonly used souring agent in Indian recipes. It lends flavour, colour and the required acidity. Sold in blocks and ready-made pastes, I prefer the paste for convenience, although it can vary in its sourness, so check your paste before using and add more or less depending on how sour it is.

Yoghurt

The recipes in this book use Greek yoghurt unless specified. Greek yoghurt is a full-fat yoghurt that is richer and creamier in texture, preventing curries from splitting. A good tip is to whisk the yoghurt before you add it to a warm curry, adding a little at a time and stirring continuously.

KITCHEN EQUIPMENT

I moved to the UK as a student two decades ago with pretty much no kitchen equipment (and no cooking skills!). Over the years, I've gathered all the equipment I need to suit my accessible, modern kitchen. If you have been cooking for a few years, chances are you will have accumulated plenty of suitable equipment for making an Indian meal.

Blender

Investing in a powerful electric blender is key for Indian cooking. The ultimate texture of a curry or chutney is usually down to how finely the paste has been ground. The size also matters: usually a small attachment ensures you won't need too much water when making the pastes, although if it is wide and large, you'll need more water to enable the blades to run better for small quantities.

Dry spice grinder

There are some really good-quality brands making small electric spice grinders. Investing in one ensures that you get a finely ground garam masala or *dhania-jeera* powder. Again, this ensures the texture of the curry you cook is smooth rather than grainy.

Pestle and mortar

I have two in my kitchen, and these grinding stones are great to coarsely crush spices or even to make a rough ginger or garlic paste. They are perfect for small quantities, too.

Pots and pans

'What pans should I use?' is a question I often get asked. I have an array in my kitchen, from stainless steel saucepans to non-stick frying pans (skillets). The key is to make sure you are investing in heavy-based pans with lids, which helps spread the heat evenly across the pan and reduce cooking times by sealing in the heat. Some of my recipes call for a *kadhai (karahi)*, a traditional Indian circular pan, often made from steel or iron and with steep sides. It is perfect for stir-frying vegetables and for the tempering of spices. If you don't have one to hand, you can use a wok.

Spice tin

I have a spice tin that I have used for years. I picked it up from Grant Road, Mumbai, at a time when I was planning on setting up my first home in Britain. A spice tin, which usually has seven-compartments, is great for everyday basic spices. I also have jars to store my other spices.

Steamer

There are a couple of recipes in this collection that use a steamer, but I would not recommend you buy one unless you plan to use it for more than just Indian cooking. If you don't have a steamer, you can simply place a trivet in the bottom of your saucepan, rest a metal colander on top, cover with a lid and bring the water to a boil.

STIR-FRIED VEGETABLES

The recipes included in this chapter are essentially a culmination of everything I have eaten on a thali at some point during my time growing up in India. Over the years, these have become the recipes I rely on for my midweek suppers. Recipes like *Achari Kaddu* (page 33) or *Tamil Keerai Poriyal* (page 38) are super quick to rustle up, with short ingredients lists. The recipes in this chapter are my go-to staples and will serve as a backbone to any thali you are planning. It is vital you have a kitty of delicious yet dependable recipes that are quick to cook, with just a few spices, reducing your overall prep time.

Stir-Fried Paneer & Peppers in a Kadhai Masala

SERVES 4

300 g (10½ oz) tomatoes, roughly chopped

2 heaped tbsp tomato purée (paste)

5 tbsp vegetable oil

80 g (3 oz) red onion, thinly sliced

300 g (10½ oz) mixed (bell) peppers, thinly sliced

450 g (1 lb) paneer, cut into bite-sized cubes

1 tsp cumin seeds

7.5 cm (3 in) ginger root, cut into matchsticks

120 g (4 oz) white onions, finely chopped

1 tsp Kashmiri chilli powder

¼ tsp ground turmeric

1 tsp ground coriander

pinch of sugar

salt, to taste

2 tbsp *kasoori methi*

chopped coriander (cilantro), to garnish

For the *kadhai* masala

3 dried red Kashmiri chillies

2 tbsp coriander seeds

2 tsp cumin seeds

1 tsp whole black peppercorns

7–8 green cardamom pods, seeds only

This recipe is a staple in my home. Paneer soaks up all the goodness of the spices, and it is perfect served with parathas or pulao. The *kadhai* masala blend quantities are enough to make this recipe twice over, so store the remainder in an airtight container for the next time you cook this dish.

First make the *kadhai* masala. Put the spices in a dry frying pan (skillet) and dry-roast over a low heat for 3–4 minutes until fragrant, stirring well to make sure they are evenly toasted. Leave to cool, then grind in a spice grinder to a coarse mix. Set aside.

Put the tomatoes and tomato purée in a blender and blend to a smooth, fine paste. Set aside.

Heat 2 tablespoons of the oil in a large frying pan over a medium heat, then add the red onion and peppers and fry for 5 minutes until they begin to soften, stirring well. Add the diced paneer, along with 3 tablespoons of the *kadhai* masala (or a touch more if you prefer it spicy). Stir well, but make sure not to break up the paneer. Cook for 2 minutes to soften, then turn off the heat and set aside.

Heat the remaining 3 tablespoons of oil in a wok or *kadhai* over a medium heat. Add the cumin seeds and two-thirds of the ginger matchsticks and fry for a few seconds, then add the white onions and fry for 12–14 minutes until they soften and change colour, stirring well to make sure they don't stick to the bottom of the pan.

Add the blended tomato purée and cook for another 12 minutes until the mixture thickens and reduces slightly. Add the chilli powder, turmeric, ground coriander and sugar, season to taste and cook for a couple of minutes, stirring well. Now add the paneer and pepper mix and stir together over a low heat for 2–3 minutes.

Turn off the heat, add the *kasoori methi* and the remaining ginger matchsticks and stir well. Garnish with fresh coriander and serve in the thali with tadka dal, *phulkas* and raita.

Pickled Squash with Turmeric & Dried Mango Powder

SERVES 4

1 tsp black mustard seeds
½ tsp fenugreek seeds
1 tsp fennel seeds
4 tbsp vegetable oil
pinch of asafoetida
5 cm (2 in) ginger root, finely chopped
750 g (1 lb 10 oz) squash or pumpkin, peeled, seeded and cut into bite-sized pieces
1 tsp Kashmiri chilli powder or mild chilli powder
½ tsp ground turmeric
salt, to taste
1 tbsp jaggery or dark soft brown sugar
2 tsp dried mango powder

Achari means 'pickling'. Cooking vegetables in pickling spices is a classic method within the north-west of India. In this recipe, the pumpkin or squash is stir-fried with whole spices, turmeric and dried mango powder, which adds the required sour flavour without any moisture.

Put the mustard, fenugreek and fennel seeds in a pestle and mortar and crush to a coarse mix, then set aside.

Heat the oil in a large frying pan (skillet) or *kadhai* over a medium heat. Add the asafoetida and the crushed spices and fry for a few seconds, then add the ginger and fry for 1 minute. Add the squash, chilli and ground turmeric, stir well and fry for 5 minutes. Add 3 tablespoons of water, season to taste and lower the heat.

Cover and continue to cook for 20 minutes, or until the squash is cooked, stirring halfway through. Crumble over the jaggery or sugar and the dried mango powder. Stir well and continue cooking for a few more minutes.

Serve warm with chapattis or naan.

Spiced Cabbage with Turmeric & Green Peas

SERVES 4

3 tbsp vegetable oil
pinch of asafoetida
2 tsp cumin seeds
2 dried mild red chillies
5–7 curry leaves
1 heaped tsp ground
　turmeric
600 g (1 lb 5 oz) white
　cabbage, thinly shredded
100 g (3½ oz) frozen green
　peas
salt, to taste
chopped coriander
　(cilantro), to garnish

Commonly known within the community as *kobi vatanachi bhaji*, this vegetarian offering is so good. The minimal use of spices keeps the dish light and perfect for a midweek meal. I prefer cooking the cabbage like my mother would, still with a slight bite to it. My favourite way to serve this dish is on the side, accompanied by a bowl of warm dal, yoghurt and freshly-cooked chapattis topped with ghee.

Heat the oil in a deep non-stick sauté pan over a medium heat. Add the asafoetida and cumin seeds and, as they begin to sputter, tip in the dried chillies and curry leaves. Stir and fry for a few seconds. Add the turmeric and stir again.

Stir in the shredded cabbage and fry well for 4–5 minutes, stirring continuously. Add the peas and a dash of water (if required) to create some moisture. Season to taste, then cover and reduce the heat. Cook for a further 3–4 minutes. The cabbage should be completely cooked, but still retain a slight bite.

Turn off the heat, leave to rest for a few minutes, then garnish with fresh coriander and serve with dal and chapattis.

Smoked Aubergines with Mustard, Chilli & Lime

SERVES 4

550 g (1 lb 3 oz) aubergines (eggplants), whole
2 tbsp mustard oil
50 g (2 oz) white onion, finely chopped
2 small green bird's-eye chillies, finely chopped
2 garlic cloves, finely chopped
100 g (3½ oz) tomatoes, finely chopped
2 tbsp finely chopped coriander (cilantro)
juice of ½ lime
salt, to taste

Mustard oil is a classic east Indian ingredient that creates a delicious pungent taste. Roasting the aubergines gives them a wonderful smoky flavour, and although I prefer doing it over an open flame, it can also be done in the oven.

Roast the aubergines for 25–30 minutes over an open flame on a medium to high heat on a gas hob. Keep turning every few minutes using a pair of tongs, being very careful as you turn. They will begin to char and soften nicely. To do this in an oven, prick the aubergines lightly with a fork, place on a baking tray and roast at 200°C fan (425°F/gas 7) for 20–25 minutes, until soft. Allow to cool slightly.

Set the roasted aubergines over a plate and peel off the skin, gently scooping out the flesh into a bowl, and mash lightly. While the flesh is still warm, add 1 tablespoon of the mustard oil, along with the onion and chillies, and leave to marinate while you fry everything else.

Heat the remaining oil in a small frying pan (skillet) over a high heat for 1 minute, letting it smoke. Cool slightly, reduce the heat to medium, then add the garlic and fry for a few seconds.

Add the tomatoes and cook for 2–3 minutes until soft, then stir in the fresh coriander. Turn off the heat and mix well. Gently combine the cooked tomato mixture to the mashed aubergines and stir well.

To finish, squeeze over the lime juice and season to taste. Allow to rest for half an hour before serving.

Spicy Stir-Fried Garlic Potatoes

SERVES 4

- 700 g (1 lb 9 oz) floury potatoes, such as Roosters, boiled and cooled
- 8 garlic cloves
- 1 tsp cumin seeds
- 10–12 curry leaves
- 3 green bird's-eye chillies
- 3 tbsp vegetable oil
- pinch of asafoetida
- 1 tsp ground turmeric
- 1 tsp sugar
- salt, to taste
- juice of ½ lemon
- chopped coriander (cilantro), to garnish

If there is one dish I grew up eating that I absolutely loved, it's *puri bhaaji*. Waiting in the queue on the bustling Mumbai streets with my mum for the street hawker to serve us a simple thali with this bhaaji, crispy fried puris, *shrikhand* and pickle on the side was always the highlight of the day. This *batata* mix is (dare I say!) the soul of Mumbai city – stir-fried potatoes with garlic, green chilli and turmeric.

Peel the boiled potatoes and roughly crush them. Set aside.

Put the garlic, cumin seeds, curry leaves and green chillies in a pestle and mortar and pound the mix to a coarse paste – the rougher the better! Set aside.

Heat the oil in a heavy-based, non-stick saucepan or *kadhai*, over a medium heat. Add the garlic and spice paste along with the asafoetida and fry for a few seconds, stirring well. Reduce the heat to low and add the turmeric, sugar and crushed potatoes, mixing well.

Season to taste, then cover and cook for 1–2 minutes. Turnoff the heat, squeeze over the lemon juice and garnish with fresh coriander.

Serve with puris, dal and a pickle of your choice.

Stir-Fried Spinach with Ginger & Coconut

SERVES 4

3 tbsp vegetable oil
handful of cashew nuts
1 dried mild red chilli
1 heaped tsp black
   mustard seeds
1 tsp urad dal (skinned and
   split variety)
10–12 curry leaves
110 g (3¾ oz) white onions,
   finely chopped
½ tsp Kashmiri chilli
   powder or mild chilli
   powder
400 g (14 oz) spinach
   leaves, washed and
   chopped
70 g (2¼ oz) grated fresh
   or frozen coconut
salt, to taste
chopped coriander
   (cilantro), to garnish

Give me a plate of *keerai poriyal* with ghee rice and I'm a happy girl. The flavour of the stir-fried spinach cooked with coconut, cashew, ginger and curry leaves is vibrant and so very delicious.

Heat 1 tablespoon of the oil in a *kadhai*, wok or large frying pan (skillet), over a medium heat and fry the cashew nuts for 3–4 minutes. Transfer to a bowl using a slotted spoon and set aside.

In the same pan heat the remaining oil over a medium heat. Add the dried chilli and fry for a few seconds, then add the mustard seeds and fry until they begin to sputter.

Add the urad dal and half the curry leaves, followed by the chopped onions, and fry for 8 minutes until the onions are beginning to soften, but not getting too much colour. Add the chilli powder and stir well.

Now add the spinach, a little at a time, making sure you stir and mix all the spices with the spinach leaves. Fry the spinach for 6–7 minutes. Season well.

Reduce the heat to low and add the coconut, along with the remaining curry leaves and the fresh coriander. Stir well and serve warm with some rice or paratha.

Malabar Spiced Cauliflower with Ginger & Curry Leaves

SERVES 4

3 tbsp vegetable oil
2 tsp mustard seeds
12–15 curry leaves
5 cm (2 in) ginger root,
 finely chopped
650 g (1 lb 7 oz) cauliflower
 florets
150 ml (5 fl oz/scant
 ⅔ cup) water
salt, to taste
280 g (10 oz) potatoes,
 cubed and boiled
½ tsp coarsely ground
 black pepper
2 tbsp finely chopped
 coriander (cilantro)

Visiting my friend Ravi's *patti* – his grandmother – in Kerala, years ago, was probably one of the best cooking experiences and life lessons I have ever had. Her approach to using vegetables, spices and techniques continues to ring true in a lot of what I do. I shared one of her recipes in my previous cookbook, and this is another of those simple yet marvellous dishes she rustled up for me. As much as this is an everyday recipe, don't let the ease of it fool you in terms of taste. The flavours are a delight, with a robust infusion of gingery curry leaves that soaks into the cauliflower and potatoes.

Heat the oil in a heavy-based saucepan over a medium heat, then add the mustard seeds and let them sputter for 5 seconds. Add half the curry leaves, along with the ginger and fry for 20 seconds. Add the cauliflower and fry for another 4 minutes. Add the water and season to taste.

Cover, reduce the heat and cook for 12 minutes, stirring halfway through to make sure it doesn't stick to the bottom of the pan. Add the pre-boiled potatoes and black pepper and simmer for a further 4–5 minutes, without the lid, until the cauliflower is cooked, stirring well so it doesn't stick. Most of the water should have reduced at this stage.

Turn off the heat and add the remaining curry leaves, along with the fresh coriander. Serve warm, with freshly cooked chapattis and some dal.

Spicy Cauliflower with Chilli & Tomato

SERVES 4

2 tbsp ghee
1 tsp cumin seeds
1 tbsp coriander seeds, coarsely crushed
1 dried mild red chilli
1 green bird's-eye chilli, slit lengthways (don't slit all the way through)
150 g (5 oz) white onions, finely chopped
6 garlic cloves, finely chopped
½ tsp Kashmiri chilli powder
1 tsp ground turmeric
160 g (5½ oz) tomatoes, finely chopped
550 g (1 lb 3 oz) cauliflower, cut into bite-sized florets
salt to taste
5 cm (2 in) ginger root, cut into matchsticks
1 tsp chaat masala
chopped coriander (cilantro), to garnish

During my travels to the scenic city of Udaipur, I had the opportunity to visit local families and chefs, who were kind enough to share their recipes. This simple cauliflower stir-fry has so much flavour; a reminder of how, with the minimum amount of ingredients, you can get wonderful aromatic flavours in these vegetarian dishes that are the heart of their region's cuisine. Ghee is commonly used in the north-west regions, but you can use vegetable oil if you prefer.

Heat the ghee in a heavy-based, non-stick saucepan over a medium heat. Add the cumin seeds, crushed coriander seeds and dried chilli and fry for a few seconds, then add the green chilli and onions, stir well and soften for 7 minutes. Add the garlic and stir for 1 minute. Now add the chilli powder and turmeric, along with the tomatoes, and fry for 5 minutes as the tomatoes soften.

Add the cauliflower florets, season to taste and mix well for 1 minute, stirring to make sure the florets are coated with the masala. Reduce the heat to low, cover and cook for 10–12 minutes until the cauliflower is cooked through, stirring halfway through.

Turn off the heat, and add the ginger matchsticks, chaat masala and fresh coriander. Stir and serve warm with dal, rotis and raita.

Spicy Sweetcorn with Ginger & Green Chilli

SERVES 4

520 g (1 lb 2 oz) tin of
  sweetcorn, drained
3 tbsp vegetable oil
pinch of asafoetida
1 heaped tsp black
  mustard seeds
1 tsp ground turmeric
salt, to taste
1 tbsp finely chopped
  coriander (cilantro)
1 tbsp roasted peanuts,
  crushed
juice of ½ lime

For the chilli and ginger paste
1 green bird's-eye chilli
3 garlic cloves, roughly
  chopped
5 cm (2 in) ginger root,
  roughly chopped

Stir-fried sweetcorn with ginger, green chilli and turmeric. Simple quick and delicious, this stir-fry is a must to accompany every thali. I've used tinned sweetcorn for this recipe, which is readily available.

First make the chilli and ginger paste by placing all the ingredients into a blender, along with 3 tablespoons of the sweetcorn, and blitz to a coarse paste. Set aside.

Heat the oil in a large frying pan (skillet) over a medium heat. Add the asafoetida and mustard seeds, and fry for a few seconds until they sputter.

Add the prepared chilli and ginger paste and fry for 1 minute, stirring well. Add the turmeric and stir, then add the remaining sweetcorn and fry for 2 minutes. Reduce the heat to low, season, and add the fresh coriander and crushed peanuts. Cover and cook for 1 more minute. Finish with the lime juice and serve warm.

Bengali Five-Spice Stir-Fried Vegetables

SERVES 4

2 tsp black mustard seeds
1 heaped tsp white poppy
　seeds
1 tsp cumin seeds
80 g (3 oz) white onion,
　chopped
4 garlic cloves
2.5 cm (1 in) ginger root
3 tbsp vegetable oil or
　mustard oil
1 tsp *panch phoron* (shop-
　bought or home-made
　page 20)
2 dried bay leaves
2 dried mild red chillies
250 g (9 oz) leftover
　cauliflower stems and
　stalks, thinly sliced
200 g (7 oz) spinach leaves,
　washed
250 g (9 oz) new potatoes,
　halved or quartered
　(if they are too big)
2 tsp sugar
1 tsp ground turmeric
salt, to taste
chopped coriander
　(cilantro), to garnish

A medley of vegetable leaves or peel and stems, stir-fried with bay leaves, chilli and turmeric, this frugal dish is a perfect everyday recipe and is cooked in so many households in the east of India. You can swap the cauliflower for squash or any vegetable peeling.

Put the mustard, poppy and cumin seeds in a spice grinder and grind to a powder, then set aside.

Put the onion, garlic and ginger into a blender with a splash of water, grind to a paste, then set aside.

Heat the oil in a large, non-stick saucepan over a medium heat. Add the *panch phoron*, bay leaves and dried chillies, and fry for a few seconds, then add the onion paste and fry for another 3–4 minutes.

Add the cauliflower, spinach and potatoes (or any other vegetable of your choice) and fry for 5 minutes. Stir well, then add the ground spice mix, along with the sugar and turmeric, and season to taste.

Cover and cook over a low heat for 20–25 minutes until the vegetables are tender, stirring a couple of times to make sure it doesn't stick to the bottom of the pan. Serve garnished with fresh coriander.

Konkani Coconut & Jackfruit Stir-Fry

SERVES 4

2 tbsp ghee
1 tsp black mustard seeds
pinch of asafoetida
1 bird's-eye chilli, finely
    chopped
8–10 curry leaves
5 garlic cloves, roughly
    crushed in a pestle and
    mortar
1 tsp ground turmeric
1 tsp Kashmiri chilli powder
1 tsp ground coriander
400 g (14 oz) tin of jackfruit,
    drained and roughly
    sliced
1½ tbsp jaggery or light
    soft brown sugar
salt, to taste
40 g (1½ oz) grated fresh
    or frozen coconut
chopped coriander
    (cilantro), to garnish
juice of ½ lemon
handful of cashew nuts,
    soaked in warm water for
    30 minutes, and drained

This stir-fry is traditionally cooked with tender jackfruit, although I am using the tinned variety here. It gives a wonderful flavour mixed with curry leaves, coconut and jaggery. If your tinned jackfruit is soaked in salty brine, make sure you drain it, and season the final dish sparingly.

Heat the ghee in a large, non-stick frying pan (skillet) over a medium heat. Add the mustard seeds, asafoetida, chilli and curry leaves. As they sputter, add the crushed garlic and fry for 1 minute.

Add the turmeric, chilli powder and ground coriander, along with the jackfruit, and mix well. Add the jaggery and season to taste. Reduce the heat to low, cover and cook for 7–8 minutes.

Finally, add the grated coconut, fresh coriander, lemon juice and the drained cashew nuts. Stir well and take it off the heat. Serve warm, with dal, pickle and chapatti.

CHICKEN CURRIES

The recipes in this chapter have got to be my favourites. They truly celebrate the regionality of India and its cuisine, yet they're accessible for our modern lifestyle. I have been cooking most of these recipes for over two decades, and it feels fitting to share the dishes my family and friends have savoured over the years. One of my go-to family recipes is the *Tariwalla Murgh* (page 52), which I love to include when putting together a thali at home. A lot of the recipes in this chapter use chicken on the bone that has been jointed: this is something I ask my butcher to do. If you are buying chicken from your local supermarket, you can just use chicken thighs and drumsticks on the bone.

Pomegranate & Chilli Spiced Chicken

SERVES 4

950 g (2 lb 2 oz) boneless, skinless chicken thighs, cut into bite-sized pieces
2 tbsp vegetable oil
300 g (10½ oz) white onions, thinly sliced
1 tsp garam masala
100 ml (3½ fl oz/scant ½ cup) water or chicken stock
salt, to taste
2 green bird's-eye chillies, slit lengthways
1 tbsp roughly chopped coriander (cilantro) leaves

For the pomegranate marinade

4 tbsp pomegranate powder
1 tsp Kashmiri chilli powder
1 tbsp ground coriander
6 garlic cloves, pounded to a paste
5 cm (2 in) ginger root, grated
1 tbsp vegetable oil

The use of pomegranate – as syrup, juice, powder and seeds – has been a prevalent part of Indian cooking for decades. With the influences of the Persian empire, this ingredient works well with spices and lends a sour note, along with a deep, rich colour. This Punjabi recipe does the fruit so much justice. The tangy pomegranate flavour works perfectly with the garlic and Kashmiri chilli powder. Pomegranate powder lends texture, and thickens the dish as well. The tanginess of the flavour can vary, so although I have used 4 tablespoons, you can decrease the quantity if your powder is quite sharp.

First make the marinade by mixing all the marinade ingredients together in a bowl. Smear the mixture over the chicken pieces and leave to marinate in the fridge for 3–4 hours or overnight.

When you're ready to cook, heat the oil in a large, non-stick frying pan (skillet) over a medium heat. Fry the onions for 11–12 minutes, until they soften and turn light brown.

Tip in the marinated chicken pieces and fry, sealing the meat, then continue to stir-fry for 5 minutes until the chicken is browned. Add the garam masala and stir well. Now add the water or stock, then season and bring to the boil.

Reduce the heat to low, letting the mixture simmer gently. Cover the pan and cook for 9–10 minutes until the chicken is cooked through, stirring halfway through.

Add the green chillies and fresh coriander. Stir and serve warm with paratha or rice.

Green Chilli Chicken Curry with Turmeric & Garam Masala

SERVES 4

1 heaped tbsp Greek yoghurt
½ tsp garam masala
600 g (1 lb 5 oz) skinless chicken on the bone, jointed
5 garlic cloves, roughly chopped
5 cm (2 in) ginger root, roughly chopped
6–7 small green bird's-eye chillies, deseeded (use up to 4 if you prefer it less spicy)
100 g (3½ oz) coriander (cilantro) leaves and stems, roughly chopped
3 tbsp vegetable oil
2 bay leaves
2.5 cm (1 in) cinnamon stick
150 g (5 oz) white onions, finely chopped
1 tsp tomato purée (paste)
½ tsp ground turmeric
1 tbsp ground coriander
salt, to taste
juice of ½ lemon

Don't be alarmed by the quantity of green chillies here. They lend depth to this dish, and combine with the fresh coriander to give a rich, flavoursome gravy. There is no chilli powder in this recipe, so the green chillies bring the required heat to the curry.

Put the yoghurt and garam masala in a large mixing bowl. Add the chicken and stir until well coated, then leave to marinate in the fridge for 2 hours or overnight.

Put the garlic and ginger in a blender with a splash of water and blend to a smooth paste, then set aside. Now put the green chillies and fresh coriander into the same blender, along with about 3 tablespoons of water, and blend to a smooth paste. Set aside.

When you are ready to cook, heat the oil in a heavy-based, non-stick saucepan over a medium heat. Add the bay leaves and cinnamon stick, and when they start to sizzle, add the onions. Fry for 10 minutes, stirring well so they colour evenly, then add the garlic and ginger paste and fry for another minute, stirring.

Add the tomato purée, turmeric and ground coriander and fry for 1 minute. Now add the marinated chicken pieces, stir well and fry for 6–7 minutes as they seal and become coated in the masala. Season to taste, then reduce the heat to low, cover and cook for 25 minutes. Stir a couple of times during the cooking process, making sure it doesn't stick to the bottom of the pan.

Finally add the chilli and coriander paste, along with about 3 tablespoons of water, and simmer for a further 5 minutes. Finish with a squeeze of lemon juice and serve with your thali.

TARIWALLA MURGH
Home-Style Chicken Curry

180 g (6½ oz) white onions, roughly chopped
6 garlic cloves, roughly chopped
2.5 cm (1 in) ginger root, roughly chopped
120 g (4 oz) tomatoes, roughly chopped
1 heaped tbsp tomato purée (paste)
3 tbsp vegetable oil
5 green cardamom pods, whole
2.5 cm (1 in) cinnamon stick
2 dried bay leaves
1 tsp ground turmeric
½ tsp Kashmiri chilli powder
1 tsp ground cumin
2 tsp ground coriander
850 g (1 lb 13 oz) skinless chicken on the bone, jointed
salt, to taste
270 ml (9 fl oz/generous 1 cup) water
230 g (8 oz) potatoes, peeled and diced
chopped coriander (cilantro), to garnish
1 tbsp lemon juice

Simple and comforting, a classic chicken curry was always part of our thalis when I was growing up. Add some bread, rice, raita or salad, and you have one of the most delicious meals. This recipe uses easy-to-find ingredients and is a favourite on days when I miss home. The key is to blend the onions separately from the garlic and ginger; the temptation is to blend them together, but the cooking times vary for each.

Place the onions into a blender and blend to a smooth paste, then remove and set aside. In the same blender, blend the garlic and ginger, then remove and set aside. Now add the tomatoes and tomato purée to the blender and blitz to a smooth paste, then set aside.

Heat the oil in a large, heavy-based, non-stick saucepan over a medium heat. Add the whole spices, and when they sizzle, add the onion paste and fry for 9–10 minutes, stirring well.

Next add the garlic and ginger paste, and fry for 1 minute as the raw flavours cook out. Add the ground tomato paste and fry for another 2 minutes. It will begin to thicken. At this stage, add the turmeric, chilli powder, cumin and ground coriander, and fry for 3 minutes, stirring well.

Add the chicken and mix to coat with all the spices, frying for 7–8 minutes to seal on all sides. Season to taste, then add the water. Bring to the boil, then cover and simmer for 15 minutes.

Add the potatoes and continue cooking, with the lid on, for another 15–17 minutes, until the potatoes are done and the chicken is cooked through. Garnish with the fresh coriander and squeeze over the lemon juice. Serve with fresh roti or pulao and a salad.

ANDHRA KODI VEPUDU

Cardamom, Ginger & Black Pepper Chicken

SERVES 4

2.5 cm (1 in) ginger root, roughly chopped
5 garlic cloves, roughly chopped
450 g (1 lb) boneless, skinless chicken thighs, cut into bite-sized pieces
3 tbsp vegetable oil
5 green cardamom pods, whole
6 cloves
10 curry leaves
80 g (3 oz) white onion, finely chopped
160 g (5½ oz) tomatoes, finely chopped
¼ tsp ground turmeric
1 tsp Kashmiri chilli powder or mild chilli powder
1 tbsp ground coriander
½ tsp coarsely ground black pepper
salt, to taste
handful of toasted cashew nuts, roughly crushed

As recipes from the Andhra region go, this is a revelation! Simple, quick and so delicious. Using boneless chicken thighs keeps the flavour and moisture of the meat intact, while allowing it to soak up all the goodness of the spices. Coarsely crushed pepper has a different flavour to ground, so add a touch more if you prefer your curry spicy.

Put the ginger and garlic into a blender, along with a splash of water, and blend to a smooth, fine paste. Put the paste into a large mixing bowl then add the chicken. Mix well, then marinate in the refrigerator for up to an hour, or preferably overnight.

When you are ready to cook, heat the oil in a wok or *kadhai* over a medium heat. Add the cardamom and cloves, letting them sizzle for a few seconds, then add half of the curry leaves, along with the onion and fry for 8 minutes, until caramelised and brown in colour.

Add the tomatoes and continue to fry for 5 minutes until they begin to soften. Stir well. Increase the heat a little and add the chicken, along with the turmeric, chilli powder and ground coriander. Stir well and seal the meat for 4 minutes. Reduce the heat to medium, then add the black pepper and season to taste. Cover and cook for 5 minutes, then remove the lid and continue cooking for another 6–7 minutes, stirring a few times until ieverything is cooked through and the masala is coating the chicken.

Turn off the heat and garnish with the remaining curry leaves, the crushed cashew nuts and a little extra black pepper. Serve with paratha.

BENGALI CHICKEN CHAAP
Creamy Saffron & Yoghurt Chicken Curry

SERVES 4

50 g (2 oz) cashew nuts

2 heaped tbsp white poppy seeds

100 ml (3½ fl oz/scant ½ cup) hot water

150 g (5 oz) white onions, roughly chopped

6 garlic cloves, roughly chopped

4 cm (1½ in) ginger root, roughly chopped

2 tbsp Greek yoghurt

1½ tsp Kashmiri chilli powder or mild paprika

1 heaped tsp ground coriander

1½ tsp saffron, soaked in 2 tbsp warm water

1 kg (2 lb 4 oz) skinless chicken on the bone, jointed

3 tbsp ghee or oil

salt, to taste

chopped coriander (cilantro), to garnish

For the spice powder

2 blades of mace

4 green cardamom pods, seeds only

3 cloves

5 cm (2 in) cinnamon stick, broken, or cassia bark

Saffron, yoghurt and chilli make the texture and taste in a chicken *chaap* creamy and delicious, with the addition of ginger and mace making it the perfect combination. I still reminisce about eating this dish in a Bengali family home almost 25 years ago. I couldn't wait to get back home to try cooking it myself. Served with a biryani, alongside a lovely feast, you could also eat this *chaap* with naan or roti, although for me, it's perfect even with a simple plate of pulao.

Crush the ingredients for the spice powder in a spice grinder, then set aside. Soak the cashew nuts and white poppy seeds in the hot water for 30 minutes.

Meanwhile, put the onions, garlic and ginger in a blender and blend to a smooth, thick paste. Set aside in a large bowl. Now, in the same blender, blend the cashew nuts and poppy seeds, along with their soaking liquid, to a smooth, thick purée, then mix this with the onion paste.

Add the yoghurt, chilli powder, ground coriander and saffron to the mixing bowl. Mix well and add the chicken pieces to the marinade. Leave to marinate in the fridge for 2 hours or overnight.

When you are ready to cook, heat the ghee or oil in a large, heavy-based, non-stick saucepan over a medium heat. Shake off the excess marinade from the chicken pieces and add them to the hot pan. Fry well on all sides for 5–7 minutes, stirring so you seal the meat evenly all over. Add the remaining marinade and stir well. Season to taste.

Cover and simmer over a low heat for 25 minutes, stirring halfway through and making sure it doesn't stick to the bottom of the pan. Now add the spice powder and continue simmering for a further 8–10 minutes.

Garnish with fresh coriander and serve with naan, roti or pulao.

CHICKEN CURRIES

Spicy Chicken Curry with Coconut & Chilli

SERVES 4

3 tbsp vegetable oil
1 tsp Kashmiri chilli powder
1 tsp ground turmeric
800 g (1 lb 12 oz) skinless chicken on the bone, jointed and
salt, to taste
400 ml (13 fl oz/generous 1½ cups) water
100 ml (3½ fl oz/scant ½ cup) coconut milk
2 tbsp lime juice

For the coconut paste
150 g (5 oz) grated fresh or frozen coconut
1 tbsp vegetable oil
250 g (9 oz) white onions, thinly sliced
4 garlic cloves, roughly chopped
2.5 cm (1 in) ginger root, roughly chopped
2 tbsp chopped coriander (cilantro) leaves and stems, plus extra to serve
150 ml (5 fl oz/scant ⅔ cup) water

For the ground spice mix
6 dried red Kashmiri chillies, deseeded
½ tsp black peppercorns
2 tbsp coriander seeds
2 star anise
6 cloves
½ tsp black mustard seeds
5 cm (2 in) cinnamon stick
½ tsp caraway seeds
½ tsp cumin seeds
1 tbsp fennel seeds
1 tsp ground nutmeg

A hearty chicken curry that's full of flavour from the coconut, chilli and lime juice, and brimming with classic spices synonymous with the west of India. Traditionally, this chicken curry is made in clay pots, which give a wonderful earthy, smoky flavour to the final dish.

First prepare your spice mix. Add all the spice mix ingredients to a large frying pan (skillet) and dry roast over a medium heat for 8–10 minutes, stirring the spices continuously. As they begin to deepen in colour and the aromas of the spices are released, turn off the heat and leave to cool. Once cool, blitz the spices in a spice grinder, until they resemble a fine powder, then set aside.

To make the coconut paste, add the grated coconut to the same frying pan, without any oil, and dry roast over a low heat for 15–20 minutes. The coconut will turn light brown and dry out slightly. Transfer the coconut to a plate and set aside, then add the oil to the pan, along with the onions, garlic, ginger and fresh coriander. Mix well and continue to fry for 10 minutes over a medium heat. The onions and garlic will brown slightly and soften. Leave the mixture to cool, then transfer to a blender, along with the coconut and water, and grind to a smooth, fine paste.

To cook the curry, heat the oil in a large, heavy-based saucepan over a medium heat. Add the coconut paste and fry for 2–3 minutes, then add the chilli powder and ground turmeric along with the ground spice mix. Fry for 1 minute, stirring well. Increase the heat slightly and add the chicken pieces. Fry for 5 minutes, mixing well as the chicken seals. Season to taste, then add the water. Bring to the boil, then cover and simmer over a low heat for 25 minutes, stirring halfway through. Add the coconut milk and simmer for a further 5 minutes until the curry thickens slightly.

To finish, squeeze in the lime juice, garnish with extra coriander, and serve with chapatti or millet bread and onion salad.

Goan Chicken Curry with a Classic *xacuti* paste

SERVES 4

900 g (2 lb) skinnless
    chicken legs and thighs,
    on the bone
pinch of salt
1 tsp ground turmeric
3 tbsp vegetable oil
230 g (8 oz) onions,
    thinly sliced
1 tsp Kashmiri chilli powder
    or mild chilli powder
300 ml (10 fl oz/1¼ cups)
    water
½ tsp ground nutmeg
1½ tbsp tamarind paste
chopped coriander
    (cilantro), to garnish

For the *xacuti* paste
120 g (4 oz) grated fresh
    coconut
6–8 dried red Kashmiri
    chillies, broken into small
    pieces, or any dried mild
    chillies
2 tbsp coriander seeds
5 cm (2 in) cinnamon stick,
    broken into small pieces
1 tsp black peppercorns
1 tsp cumin seeds
1 tsp fennel seeds
4 cloves
2 star anise
1 heaped tbsp white poppy
    seeds
6 garlic cloves, roughly
    chopped
120 ml (4 fl oz/½ cup) water

Pronounced 'shakooti', this dish is one you'll find all across the Goan landscape. The ground paste, made with coconut, black pepper, poppy seeds and chilli, is where the secret to making a good *xacuti* lies. This recipe has been shared by the landlady of the Portuguese guest house I frequented years ago.

Put the chicken pieces in a bowl. Sprinkle with the salt and turmeric and mix together, then set aside while you prepare the spice paste.

To make the *xacuti* paste, heat a frying pan (skillet) over a low heat. Add the grated coconut and dry roast for 12–14 minutes until it starts to brown, then transfer to a plate and set aside. Return the pan to the heat and add the remaining ingredients except for the poppy seeds, garlic and water. Dry roast for 5 minutes, stirring well to make sure all the spices are heated and start to give out a spicy aroma. At this stage, add the poppy seeds and roast for a further 3 minutes. Turn off the heat and allow the mixture to cool, then transfer to a blender, along with the garlic. Add half of the water and blitz before adding the remaining water, a little at a time, to make a thick, finely ground paste. You don't want to add too much water.

To make the curry, heat the oil in a heavy-based saucepan and add the sliced onions. Fry over a medium heat for 14–15 minutes until they soften and start to brown. Add the spice paste and stir-fry for a further 5 minutes, making sure it doesn't stick to the bottom of the pan. Increase the heat slightly, then add the chilli powder, along with about 3 tablespoons of water to loosen the spices from the bottom of the pan.

Add the chicken pieces and stir to coat in the spice paste. Fry for 5 minutes, turning to seal the meat all over. Now add the remaining water, stir, and bring to the boil. Season to taste, then reduce the heat to low, cover and simmer for 20 minutes until the chicken pieces are tender, stirring halfway through. Add the nutmeg and tamarind paste and cook for a further 7–8 minutes without the lid. Garnish with coriander and serve with *pav* bread (or bread rolls) or steamed plain basmati rice.

CHICKEN CURRIES

PARSI KAJU MA MURGI
Parsi Creamy Chicken Curry

SERVES 4

10–12 dried red Kashmiri chillies, deseeded and soaked in 100 ml (3½ fl oz/scant ½ cup) warm water

50 g (2 oz) cashew nuts, soaked in 100 ml (3½ fl oz/scant ½ cup) warm water

6 garlic cloves, roughly chopped

5 cm (2 in) ginger root, roughly chopped

1 tsp cumin seeds

2 tsp fennel seeds

2 tbsp vegetable oil

4 whole cloves

1 bay leaf

6 green cardamom pods, whole

180 g (6½ oz) white onions, finely chopped

900 g (2 lb) skinless chicken on the bone, jointed

200 ml (7 fl oz/scant 1 cup) water

salt, to taste

2 tsp sugar

1 tbsp chopped coriander (cilantro), to garnish

Cooked in a cashew paste with spices and coriander, a lot of Persian influences are prevalent in dishes like this. It is often served at Parsi weddings during the wedding feast, which is known as a *bhonu*.

Let the chillies and cashew nuts soak in their separate bowls of warm water for at least 30 minutes.

Put the garlic, ginger, cumin and fennel seeds in a blender, along with the soaked chillies and 3 tablespoons of the chilli-soaking water. Blend to form a thick paste, then set aside. Blend the cashew nuts separately with 3–5 tablespoons of their soaking water to form a thick paste, and set aside.

Heat the oil in a heavy-based saucepan over a medium heat. Add the cloves, bay leaf and cardamom pods and fry for a few seconds until they start to sputter. Add the onions and cook, stirring frequently, for 12–14 minutes until they soften and turn light brown. Tip in the garlic, ginger, cumin, fennel and chilli paste and stir for 2–3 minutes, cooking out the raw flavours. Add the chicken to the pan and fry for 7–8 minutes, sealing the meat and letting the spice mix coat it thoroughly. Add the water and season to taste. Cover and cook over a low heat for 25–30 minutes.

Remove the lid and add the sugar and ground cashew nut paste. Simmer without the lid for a further 4–5 minutes until the chicken is cooked through and the gravy has thickened. Garnish with fresh coriander and serve.

Stir-Fried Chicken with Whole Spices & Green Chillies

SERVES 4

1 green bird's-eye chilli
5 garlic cloves, roughly
   chopped
5 cm (2 in) ginger root,
   roughly chopped
4 tbsp vegetable oil or
   mustard oil
300 g (10½ oz) white
   onions, thinly sliced
150 g (5 oz) tomatoes,
   roughly chopped
1 tbsp ground coriander
900 g (2 lb) skinless chicken
   on the bone, jointed and
   cut into medium-sized
   pieces
salt, to taste
½ tsp garam masala
1 tbsp roughly chopped
   coriander (cilantro),
   to garnish

For the whole-spice mix
5 cm (2 in) cassia bark
2 dried bay leaves
1 tsp black peppercorn
1 black cardamom pod,
   whole
1 tsp cumin seeds
8 cloves

I have very fond memories of my visits to Jaipur and Udaipur, tucking into hearty dishes like this. Whole spices are coarsely crushed and fried to infuse the oil, then onions and ginger are cooked with chicken on the bone. This particular dry-fry dish is a personal favourite. The caramelised onions coat the chicken, along with coarsely crushed bay leaves, cinnamon and cardamom, lending a warmth to the final dish. Ideally, it would be served on your thali with plain dal, parathas and some cucumber salad.

First make the whole-spice mix. Add all the ingredients to a pestle and mortar and pound to a coarse mix. You might have some that isn't crushed completely, but that's fine. Set aside.

Put the green chilli, garlic and ginger in a blender and blitz to a smooth, fine paste with a splash of water. Set aside.

Heat the oil in a large, heavy-based saucepan over a medium heat. Add the crushed whole-spice mix and fry for a couple of seconds, then add the onions and fry for 12–14 minutes until they are beginning to soften. Stir every few minutes, making sure they don't stick to the bottom of the pan. Add the chilli, ginger and garlic paste and fry for 1–2 minutes. Add a splash of water and scrape off the bottom of the pan; mix well as everything turns a rich, dark colour.

Add the chopped tomatoes and continue to fry for 3–4 minutes until they begin to soften, mashing them lightly with the back of the spoon. Add the ground coriander and stir, then add the chicken and combine well. Season to taste and cook for 6 minutes, stirring to coat the chicken pieces in the masala.

Reduce the heat to low, cover and continue cooking for 25 minutes, making sure to stir halfway through. The chicken will begin to release its juices and cook in its own stock, so there is no water required. If it does get too dry, add about 3 tablespoons of water, but only if needed. Turn off the heat and add the garam masala and garnish with fresh coriander. Stir well and serve warm with roti or naan and cucumber raita.

Green Mango, Mint & Coconut Chicken Curry

SERVES 4

2 garlic cloves, roughly chopped

5 cm (2 in) ginger root, roughly chopped

3 tbsp vegetable oil

150 g (5 oz) white onions, finely chopped

2 green bird's-eye chillies, slit lengthways

750 g (1 lb 10 oz) skinless chicken on the bone, jointed

salt, to taste

200 ml (7 fl oz/scant 1 cup) water

120 g (4 oz) mango, diced into bite-sized chunks

juice of ½ lime

For the green chutney paste

180 g (6½ oz) mango, diced

50 g (2 oz) coriander (cilantro) leaves and stems

25 g (1 oz) mint leaves

2 garlic cloves

50 g (2 oz) grated fresh or frozen coconut

100 ml (3½ fl oz/scant ½ cup) water

Mint, fresh mango and chicken come together in this gorgeous Parsi dish. It is a favourite of the community and is often served during celebrations. I use ripe mangoes, but if you are able to get hold of green, unripe mangoes, those work really well, giving a lovely sour flavour to the curry. Add a pinch of sugar to the gravy to balance the flavours.

First make the green chutney paste. Place all the paste ingredients into a blender and blitz to form a smooth paste. Remove from the blender and set aside. In the same blender, grind the garlic and ginger with a splash of water. Set aside.

Heat the oil in a heavy-based saucepan over a medium heat. Add the onions and fry for 10–12 minutes until they begin to brown. Add the garlic and ginger paste and fry for 1 minute to release the raw flavours.

Add the green chillies and the chicken and fry for 2–3 minutes. Season and add the water, then reduce the heat to low and simmer for 15 minutes, stirring halfway through. Now add the green chutney paste, along with most of the diced mango and the lime juice, and simmer for 10 minutes, stirring well. Add the remaining mango and serve warm with *phulkas* or rice.

TAMIL KODI KURA

Poppy Seed & Coconut Chicken Curry

SERVES 4

4 garlic cloves
2.5 cm (1 in) ginger root
3 tbsp vegetable oil
5 cm (2 in) cinnamon stick
3 cloves
3 green cardamom pods, whole
2 bay leaves
200 g (7 oz) white onions, thinly sliced
2 green chillies, slit lengthways
900 g (2 lb) chicken on the bone, cut into medium-sized pieces
½ tsp turmeric powder
1½ tsp Kashmiri chilli powder (or mild chilli powder)
1 tbsp tomato purée (paste)
500 ml (17 fl oz/2 cups) water
salt, to taste
chopped coriander (cilantro), to garnish

For the paste
1 tbsp white poppy seeds
1 tbsp cashew nuts
70 ml (2½ fl oz scant ⅓ cup) water
3 tbsp grated fresh coconut

This coconut chicken curry, from the region of Tamil Nadu, is made with whole spices, a ground poppy-seed paste and tomatoes. I discovered it on my travels to Chennai, while visiting the Kannan family. Being restaurateurs and avid cooks, they were kind enough give me their insight into local dishes. Chennai is brimming with street markets, stalls and restaurants. Sampling a varied variety of thalis during my visits there has given me an education on the region's dishes and ingredients, and how, within a single state, they're communities that thrive through the spices and food they celebrate.

To make the paste, place the poppy seeds and cashew nuts in a small bowl. Pour over the water and leave to soak for half an hour. Transfer to a blender, along with the soaking liquid. Add the coconut and blend to a smooth paste, then remove from the blender and set aside. Put the garlic and ginger in the blender and blend to a paste. Set aside.

Heat the oil in a large, heavy-based saucepan over a medium heat. Add the whole spices and fry for 20 seconds, then add the onions and fry for 12–15 minutes as they colour and soften. Add the garlic and ginger paste, along with the green chillies, and fry for 1 minute.

Add the chicken pieces, along with the turmeric and chilli powder. Fry on a medium–high heat for 8 minutes, stirring well as the pieces begin to seal. Add the tomato purée and fry for 1 minute, then add the water. Season and bring to the boil, then cover, reduce the heat to low and simmer for 25 minutes. Now add the ground poppy-seed paste and simmer for a further 5 minutes, with the lid on.

Garnish with coriander and serve with rice or paratha.

Curry Leaf & Ghee Fried Chicken

SERVES 4

700 g (1 lb 9 oz) skinless chicken on the bone, jointed
2 tbsp Greek yoghurt
½ tsp ground turmeric
salt, to taste
3 tbsp ghee
100 g (3½ oz) white onions, finely chopped
10 curry leaves
2 tsp jaggery or light soft brown sugar
2 tbsp lemon juice

For the masala paste
6–7 dried red Kashmiri chillies or any dried mild chillies
1 tsp black peppercorns
2 tsp coriander seeds
1 tsp cumin seeds
2 tsp fennel seeds
3 garlic cloves, roughly chopped
2.5 cm (1 in) ginger root, roughly chopped
100 ml (3½ fl oz/scant ½ cup) water

A visit to Mangalore in south India is never complete without sampling this ghee-roasted chicken curry. The aromatic flavours of the crushed spices, cooked with onions in ghee make it one to be devoured.

Put the chicken in a large mixing bowl with the yoghurt, turmeric and a pinch of salt. Mix well and marinate in the fridge for 2 hours or preferably overnight.

To make the masala paste, heat a large frying pan (skillet) over a medium heat. Add the dried chillies and roast for 5 minutes. They will begin to deepen and darken in colour. Transfer to a plate and leave to cool. Add the peppercorns, coriander seeds, cumin and fennel seeds to the same pan and dry-roast for 2–3 minutes. Add the roasted chillies and spices to a blender, along with the garlic, ginger and water, and blend to form a fine, smooth paste. Set aside.

When you are ready to cook, heat the ghee in a heavy-based saucepan over a medium heat. Add the onions and fry for 8–9 minutes until they soften and begin to change colour. Add the ground masala paste and fry for 2–3 minutes until the oil begins to separate. Stir well and add the marinated chicken, along with any leftover marinade. Increase the heat slightly and stir well for 7–8 minutes, sealing the chicken pieces. Season to taste, then reduce the heat to low, cover and simmer for 20 minutes, stirring halfway through. The chicken will cook in its juices and the yoghurt marinade.

Once the chicken is cooked and the gravy has thickened slightly, add the curry leaves, jaggery and lemon juice. Stir well as the jaggery dissolves, then serve warm with rice or paratha and a fresh salad.

Spinach & Ginger Chicken Curry

SERVES 4

850 g (1 lb 13 oz) skinless chicken on the bone, cut into medium-sized pieces
400 g (14 oz) spinach leaves, washed and trimmed
4 cm (1½ in) ginger root, roughly chopped
5 garlic cloves, roughly chopped
1 green bird's-eye chilli
3 tbsp vegetable oil
4 green cardamom pods, whole
2 bay leaves
2.5 cm (1 in) cinnamon stick
250 g (9 oz) white onions, finely chopped
1 heaped tbsp tomato purée (paste)
1 heaped tsp ground coriander
salt, to taste
½ tsp garam masala
1 tbsp chopped coriander (cilantro), to garnish
ginger root, cut into matchsticks, to garnish

For the spiced yoghurt marinade
3 tbsp Greek yoghurt
1 tsp ground turmeric
1 tsp Kashmiri chilli powder or mild chilli powder
1½ tsp cumin seeds, coarsely crushed

Marrying green, leafy vegetables with meat is the hallmark of north Indian cooking. A classic *palak*, or spinach and chicken curry, is one of my favourite dishes served with pulao. This one is spiced with ginger, coriander and garam masala.

First prepare the marinade. Mix all the marinade ingredients together in a large bowl. Make a few cuts in the chicken pieces to let the marinade soak in, then add the chicken pieces to the bowl and mix well, making sure they are all coated. Leave overnight in the refrigerator – even just 30 minutes is fine.

Add the spinach to a blender with 3 tablespoons of water and blend to a smooth paste. You may need to do this in batches. Separately, blend the ginger, garlic and green chilli with 2–3 tablespoons of water to form a paste. Set aside.

Heat the oil in a heavy-based, non-stick saucepan or *kadhai*, over a medium heat. Add the whole spices and fry for a few seconds. Add the onions and fry for 15 minutes, stirring well, until the colour begins to change. Add the ginger, garlic and chilli paste and fry for a further 2 minutes, stirring. Add a splash of water if it begins to stick to the base of the pan, then add the tomato purée. Fry for a couple of minutes, then stir in the ground coriander.

Now add the marinated chicken and fry for 7–8 minutes, stirring and making sure to seal the pieces well. Reduce the heat to a low, season to taste, then cover and cook for 15–17 minutes until the chicken is cooked through, stirring halfway to make sure it doesn't stick to the bottom of the pan.

Now add the puréed spinach and continue to simmer over a low heat for a further 5–7 minutes, with the lid on. Finish with the garam masala, fresh coriander and ginger matchsticks, and stir together. Serve with naan or pulao, some raita and pickled slices of onion.

LAMB CURRIES

Anyone that knows me well knows that I absolutely love cooking a hearty lamb curry: it's slow-cooking at its best, and a pure labour of love. This is one chapter where you want to plan ahead, get your ingredients ready and take your time while cooking. Lamb on the bone lends much more flavour to the gravy, but if you prefer, you can swap it for boneless lamb. My recipe for *Rajasthani Laal Maas* (page 84) also includes bone with marrow, which gives an added layer of rich flavour to the curry. Readers often ask me why their curry is weak or thin, and my main advice would be to take your time while making the base. This way, you will get the most out of the spices and ingredients you add at every stage.

BENGALI MANGSHO GHUGNI
Slow-Cooked Lamb & Chickpea Curry

SERVES 4

4 garlic cloves
5 cm (2 in) ginger root, roughly chopped
3 tbsp vegetable oil
2 dried bay leaves
4 cloves
4 green cardamom pods, whole
250 g (9 oz) white onions, thinly sliced
2 green bird's-eye chillies, slit lengthways
1 tbsp ground coriander
1 tsp ground cumin
½ tsp Kashmiri chilli powder
200 g (7 oz) tomatoes, finely chopped
1 heaped tsp tomato purée (paste)
600 g (1 lb 5 oz) boneless leg of lamb, cut into bite-size chunks
500 ml (17 fl oz/2 cups) water
1 tsp sugar
salt, to taste
200 g (7 oz) tinned, drained chickpeas (garbanzos)
½ tsp garam masala
chopped coriander (cilantro), to garnish
red onion, finely chopped, to serve
juice of ½ lime

This recipe from the east of India is one of my favourites. The chickpeas and lamb are slow-cooked with ginger, whole spices and garam masala, which helps to form a thick, luscious gravy. Traditionally, this recipe is made with minced lamb, but here I have used boneless leg of lamb for texture and depth, as well as additional bones from my butcher, to add flavour to the gravy. But you can leave the bones out, if you wish. I prefer using tinned chickpeas, as this makes it simpler to cook.

In a blender, blend the garlic and ginger to a smooth paste, then set aside.

Heat the oil in a large, heavy-based saucepan over a medium heat. Add the bay leaves and whole spices and, as they begin to sizzle, add the white onions. Fry for 12–14 minutes, stirring often.

Add the garlic and ginger paste, along with the green chillies, and fry for a few seconds, then add the ground coriander, cumin and chilli powder and stir well. Add the tomatoes and cook for 4 minutes, scraping the bottom of the pan. Add a splash of water if it is sticking to the base. Add the tomato purée and stir well.

Now add the lamb and stir to coat in the spices, sealing the meat for 5–6 minutes. Add the water and sugar and season to taste. Bring to the boil, then cover and simmer over a low heat for 40 minutes, stirring halfway through.

Add the chickpeas, cover and continue cooking for 20–25 minutes. Stir a couple of times to make sure it doesn't stick to the bottom of the pan. Add the garam masala, fresh coriander and red onion. Turn off the heat and serve warm, sprinkled with lime juice.

Creamy Tender Lamb Curry

SERVES 4

800 g (1 lb 12 oz) leg of
  lamb on the bone, cut
  into bite-sized pieces
5 garlic cloves, blended
  to a smooth paste
1 tsp cumin seeds
3 tbsp ghee (clarified
  butter)
pinch of asafoetida
4 cloves
2 green bird's-eye chillies,
  slit lengthways
200 g (7 oz) white onions,
  blended to a smooth
  paste
600 ml (20 fl oz/2½ cups)
  water or lamb stock
salt, to taste
chopped coriander
  (cilantro), to garnish

For the yoghurt mix
280 g (10 oz/generous
  1 cup) Greek yoghurt,
  whisked
3 tbsp chickpea (gram)
  flour
1 tsp Kashmiri chilli powder
1 tsp ground turmeric
200 ml (7 fl oz/scant 1 cup)
  water

One of my favourite dishes from the north-west of India, *maas ki kadhi* is cooked in a creamy yoghurt curry. Yoghurt is commonly used in dishes within this region, as the weather has soaring temperatures and it helps keep the food fresh for longer. Yoghurt also works as a great tenderiser for the meat as it simmers in the gravy.

Put the lamb in a large mixing bowl, along with the garlic paste and stir together. Leave to marinate while you make the yoghurt mix.

Put the yoghurt ingredients in a bowl and whisk well, making sure there are no lumps. Set aside.

Next, using a pestle and mortar, crush the cumin seeds to a coarse powder and set aside.

Melt the ghee in a large, heavy-based saucepan over a medium heat and add the asafoetida, cloves and green chillies. Fry for a few seconds, then add the onion paste and fry for a further 8 minutes, stirring well and scraping up any bits that stick to the bottom of the pan.

Add the marinated lamb and fry for 10 minutes. Stir well as the lamb begins to brown and seal. Add the water or stock and season to taste. Bring to the boil, then cover and simmer over a low heat for 1 hour 20 minutes, stirring halfway through. The lamb will be tender at this stage.

Take the pan off the heat and add the yoghurt mix a little at a time, stirring or whisking continuously for 2–3 minutes, until all the yoghurt has been added. Return the pan back to a low heat and keep stirring for 5–6 minutes as the gravy thickens. Turn off the heat and add the coarsly ground cumin. Garnish with fresh coriander and serve with rice or pulao.

720 g (1 lb 9½ oz) leg of
  lamb on the bone, cut
  into bite-sized pieces
½ tsp ground turmeric
1 tsp fennel seeds
½ tsp black peppercorns
3 tbsp vegetable oil
2 green bird's-eye chillies,
  slit lengthways
160 g (5½ oz) white onions,
  thinly sliced
5 garlic cloves, sliced
5 cm (2 in) ginger root, cut
  into matchsticks
120 g (4 oz) tomatoes,
  finely chopped
1 tbsp ground coriander
½ tsp Kashmiri chilli
  powder
450 ml (15¼ fl oz/scant
  2 cups) lamb stock
  or water
salt, to taste
220 g (8 oz) potatoes,
  peeled and diced
4 green cardamom pods,
  whole
10 curry leaves
200 ml (7 fl oz/scant 1 cup)
  coconut milk
chopped coriander
  (cilantro), to garnish

ATTIRACHI PERELAN

Malabar Spicy Lamb Curry

This slow-cooked lamb curry with coconut milk and curry leaves celebrates spices from the coastal region of Kerala, including fennel and black pepper. It's one that always takes me back to my travels and my stay with the Nambiar family, who were kind enough to share this recipe with me.

Put the lamb and turmeric in a mixing bowl and mix well, then set aside while you get the curry ready.

Put the fennel seeds and black pepper in a pestle and mortar and crush to a coarse powder, then set aside.

Heat the oil in a large, heavy-based saucepan over a medium heat. Add the chillies and, when they sputter, add the onions and fry for 12 minutes, stirring well. Add the garlic and fry for 1 minute, then add the ginger matchsticks and tomatoes and fry for 3–4 minutes until the tomatoes soften.

Add the coriander and chilli powder, along with the marinated lamb, stir well and fry for 6–7 minutes to seal the meat. Add the stock or water, then eason to taste. Cover and simmer over a low heat for 45 minutes, stirring halfway through.

Add the potatoes and continue to cook for 20 minutes with the lid on until the potatoes are cooked through. Crush a few of the potatoes with the back of a spoon to thicken the gravy, then add the green cardamom, curry leaves and coconut milk, along with the crushed fennel and black pepper. Stir well and simmer for 8–10 minutes.

Garnish with fresh coriander and serve on your thali with raita, paratha or rice.

ACHARI GOSHT
Slow-Cooked Lamb Curry in Pickling Spices

SERVES 4

850 g (1 lb 14 oz) lamb shoulder on the bone, cut into bite-size pieces
pinch of salt, plus extra to taste
1 tsp ground turmeric
600 ml (20 fl oz/2½ cups) water
6 garlic cloves
2.5 cm (1 in) ginger root
1 tsp black mustard seeds
1 tsp fennel seeds
1 tsp cumin seeds
4 tbsp vegetable oil
250 g (9 oz) white onions, thinly sliced
4 dried red Kashmiri chillies or any dried mild chillies
1 black cardamom pod, whole
6 cloves
½ tsp asafoetida
2 heaped tsp mango powder
1½ tsp Kashmiri chilli powder
1 tbsp dark soft brown sugar
chopped coriander (cilantro), to garnish

This family recipe is an absolute gem. The key to this spicy yet flavoursome gravy, which is rich and slightly thick, is not using tomatoes or yoghurt. *Achar* literally means 'pickled', and this recipe uses whole spices that are synonymous with the pickling process across India.

Put the lamb, a pinch of salt, turmeric and water in a heavy-based saucepan over a medium to high heat. Bring to the boil, cover, reduce the heat to low and simmer for 30 minutes. Turn off the heat and leave to cool slightly.

Remove the lamb chunks from the stock using a slotted spoon and place in a bowl. Set the lamb and the stock to one side.

In a blender, blend the garlic and ginger with 3 tablespoons of water to make a paste, and set aside. Put the mustard seeds, fennel seeds and cumin seeds in a pestle and mortar and crush to a coarse mix, then set aside.

Heat the oil in a large, heavy-based, non-stick saucepan over a medium heat. Add the onions and fry for 17–18 minutes until they begin to turn brown. Make sure to stir and scrape off any sticky edges. Add the chillies and fry for a couple of minutes, and then add the black cardamom, cloves and crushed mustard seeds, cumin seeds and fennel seeds. Fry and stir for 1 minute. Stir in the garlic and ginger paste and fry for 10 seconds to get the raw smells to cook out.

Mix the asafoetida, mango powder and chilli powder in a bowl with 2 tablespoons of the stock and add this to the pan, stirring well, then add the boiled lamb pieces, and season to taste. Mix and fry for 2–3 minutes, before adding 450 ml (15¼ fl oz/scant 2 cups) of the lamb stock, along with the sugar. Stir well, cover and continue to simmer for 50 minutes over a low heat, stirring a couple of times during cooking to make sure it doesn't stick to the bottom of the pan. Add a little more stock only if it's too dry. You're looking for a thick gravy rather than a soupy consistency.

When ready to serve, garnish with fresh coriander and serve on a thali with a tandoori roti or naan.

Apricot Lamb Curry with Crispy Potato Straws

SERVES 4

5 cm (2 in) ginger root, roughly chopped

6 garlic cloves, roughly chopped

100 g (3½ oz) tomatoes, roughly chopped

1 tbsp tomato purée (paste)

4 tbsp vegetable oil

5 green cardamom pods, whole

6 cloves

260 g (9½ oz) white onions, thinly sliced

2 tsp Kashmiri chilli powder or mild paprika

1 tsp ground turmeric

850 g (1 lb 13 oz) lamb leg on the bone, cut into 3 cm (1¼ in) pieces

1 small green bird's-eye chilli, slit lengthways

300 ml (10 fl oz/1¼ cups) water

2 tbsp jaggery or caster sugar

4 dried apricots, finely chopped

1 tbsp malt vinegar

½ tsp cumin seeds, coarsely ground

½ tsp garam masala

shop-bought potato straws, to garnish

A celebratory dish from the Parsi community in the west of India in Mumbai, this curry is served on special occasions and at family gatherings. I've been fortunate enough to have eaten bowlfuls of this dish while growing up in Mumbai. Lamb on the bone is cooked in a lightly spiced sauce with cloves, ginger and garlic. The lamb curry is simmered with apricots and jaggery for a touch of sweetness, and served topped with potato straws (*salli*), which lend a lovely texture and crunch. You can make your own, but shop-bought ones are fine.

Put the ginger and garlic in a blender with 2 tablespoons of water and blend to a smooth paste, then remove and set aside. In the same blender, blend the tomato and tomato purée to a fine paste. Set aside.

Heat the oil in a large, heavy-based saucepan over a medium heat. Add the green cardamom and cloves, letting them sizzle for a few seconds, followed by the onions. Stir well and fry for 15–17 minutes, until the onions begin to soften and go brown. Add the ginger and garlic paste and fry for a further minute, stirring well. Add a splash of water at this stage to scrape off anything that has stuck to the bottom of the pan.

Add the Kashmiri chilli powder and turmeric and fry for a few seconds, then add the tomato mix. Stir well, mixing everything together, and fry for 2–3 minutes. Add the lamb chunks and cook for 5 minutes, making sure all the masala is coating the lamb and that the meat seals all over. Add the green chilli, along with 150 ml (5 fl oz/scant ⅔ cup) of the water. Bring to the boil then cover and simmer over a low heat for 40 minutes. Stir a few times during cooking.

Add the remaining water and continue to simmer over a low heat, with the lid on, for a further 40 minutes, making sure to stir a few times. The lamb curry should now be a darker and richer colour. Add the jaggery, apricots and vinegar, and cook for 1 minute. Turn off the heat and add the crushed cumin seeds and garam masala. Serve topped with potato straws, with some basmati rice and a simple red onion salad.

Soupy Cardamom & Black Pepper Lamb Curry

SERVES 4

1½ tsp green cardamom seeds
1 tbsp black peppercorn
4 tbsp ghee
800 g (1 lb 12 oz) shoulder of lamb on the bone, cut into bite-sized pieces
½ tsp ground turmeric
1 tbsp ground coriander
350 ml (12¼ fl oz/1½ cups) water
salt, to taste
200 g (7 oz) tomatoes, finely chopped
2 tbsp finely chopped coriander (cilantro)

Lamb on the bone slow-cooked with ground cardamom – delicious! Cardamom is not only much loved in Indian savoury dishes, but also in sweets and drinks like chai. In this soupy curry, the warmth and aroma gets better as it keeps cooking. This recipe, from the Sindhi community, is a favourite, and cooked without any onions or garlic. The main cardamom flavour lends itself to the light broth. Lots of shops and online stores sell green cardamom seeds already podded, which makes this recipe easier.

Put the cardamom seeds and black pepper in a spice grinder and grind to a powder. Set aside.

Heat the ghee in a heavy-based saucepan over a medium heat. Add the spice powder and stir for a few seconds, then add the lamb and fry for 5 minutes. Stir as it begins to seal. Add the turmeric and ground coriander and continue to fry for 5–6 minutes. Add the water, season to taste and bring to the boil.

Reduce the heat to low, cover and continue to simmer for 45 minutes, stirring halfway through. Add the tomatoes and continue cooking for a further 40 minutes as they soften and the gravy thickens. The lamb will be tender and cooked through.

When ready to eat, garnish with fresh coriander and serve warm with roti.

ANDHRA CHINTAKAYA CHAAP
Tamarind & Ginger Lamb Chop Curry

10 lamb chops
5 cm (2 in) ginger root blended to a paste (about 2 tbsp)
4 tbsp vegetable oil
450 g (1 lb) white onions, thinly sliced
1 tsp English mustard powder
½ tsp mild chilli powder
150 ml (5½ fl oz/scant ⅔ cup) water
salt, to taste
125 g (4 oz) potatoes, sliced
1 heaped tsp tamarind paste, or to taste
chopped coriander (cilantro), to garnish

Sometimes it's the simpler dishes that bring out the very best flavours in Indian cooking, and perhaps also help bust the myth that you always need a long list of ingredients to get the right flavour. This Andhra recipe for lamb chop curry is slow-cooked with chilli and sliced potato. For me, this is a true representation of Andhra cooking and, once again, shows a varied style from the region beyond fiery hot curries. Tamarind paste varies in strength, so adjust the quantity to get the required tart, sour flavour in the curry.

Put the chops in a mixing bowl with the ginger paste and marinate for a few hours or overnight.

When you are ready to cook, heat the oil in a large, heavy-based saucepan over a medium heat. Add the onions and fry for 35–40 minutes until they caramelise and turn light brown. Stir well, making sure you scrape up anything that sticks to the bottom of the pan.

Add the chops to the pan and fry for 2–3 minutes. Add the mustard powder and chilli powder and mix well, then continue to fry for 5 minutes. At this stage, add 50 ml (1¾ fl oz/3 tablespoons) of the water, then season to taste. Cover and cook for 15 minutes over a low heat.

Add the potatoes, tamarind paste and remaining 100 ml (3½ fl oz/scant ½ cup) of the water, and continue to cook for 12–14 minutes until the potatoes are cooked through. Add a little more water only if needed; you want a very light sauce for the dish. Garnish with fresh coriander and serve with rotis or parathas and *kachumber* (chopped salad).

LAMB CURRIES

Country-Style Coconut, Chilli & Fennel Lamb Curry

SERVES 4

750 g (1 lb 10 oz) lamb
  shoulder on the bone,
  cut into bite-sized pieces
3 tbsp vegetable oil
200 g (7 oz) white onions,
  thinly sliced
1 tsp ground turmeric
320 g (11 oz) tomatoes,
  roughly chopped
550 ml (18 fl oz/7¼ cups)
  water
chopped coriander
  (cilantro), to garnish

For the spice powder
10 dried red Kashmiri
  chillies, deseeded
8 cloves
5 cm (2 in) cinnamon stick
2 tsp fennel seeds
1 tsp black peppercorns
1 tbsp coriander seeds
1 tbsp white poppy seeds

For the coconut paste
200 g (7 oz) grated fresh
  or frozen coconut
5 cm (2 in) ginger root,
  roughly chopped
8 garlic cloves, roughly
  chopped
70–80 ml (about 3 fl oz/
  ⅓ cup) water

This is a recipe from my hometown of Mumbai, and one that my family has been cooking for over two decades. With influences from surrounding communities across the west of India, this recipe is cooked with coarsely crushed spices and lamb on the bone. With its rustic flavours, this *rassa* (gravy) has so much depth. Sundays are for thalis with *gavraan rassa*, chapattis, salad, *vadis* and plain rice. Of course, this is called *muttonacha*, meaning mutton, which is what my mother would use, so although I've opted for lamb, feel free to use mutton, if you wish.

First make the spice powder by placing all the spice powder ingredients, except the white poppy seeds, in a frying pan (skillet) and dry-roast over a low heat for 4–5 minutes. Stir well and as the chillies begin to darken, add the poppy seeds and toast for a further 2 minutes. Turn off the heat and leave to cool, then grind to a fine powder in a spice grinder. Put the lamb in a large mixing bowl and sprinkle the spice powder over the top. Leave to marinate in the fridge for 2–3 hours or overnight.

To make the coconut paste, toast the coconut in the same frying pan over a medium heat for 7–8 minutes, until light brown. Add the ginger and garlic and fry for 5 minutes, stirring continuously to make sure they don't burn at the bottom of the pan. Remove from the heat and add to a blender with enough of the water to blend to a thick paste. Set aside.

When you are ready to cook, heat the oil in a large, heavy-based saucepan over a medium heat. Add the onions and fry for 8–10 minutes until they begin to change colour. Add the marinated lamb pieces and the turmeric. Fry the lamb for 7–10 minutes to seal the meat well, stirring to make sure you scrape up anything that has stuck to the bottom of the pan. Add the coconut paste and mix well, frying for 5 minutes. Add the tomatoes and cook for another 2 minutes. Now add the water and season to taste. Stir well, bring to the boil, cover and simmer over a low heat for 50 minutes, stirring occasionally. Continue simmering for a further 30 minutes until the lamb is tender and the gravy has thickened. Garnish with fresh coriander and serve on your thali with salad, raita and *phulkas*.

RAJASTHANI LAAL MAAS
Spiced Bone Marrow Lamb Curry

SERVES 4

8 garlic cloves, roughly chopped

5 cm (2 in) ginger root, roughly chopped

750 g (1 lb 10 oz) lamb shoulder, diced into bite-sized pieces

1½ tsp Kashmiri chilli powder or mild chilli powder

10 dried red Kashmiri chillies, soaked in 400 ml (13 fl oz/generous 1½ cups) warm water

120 ml (4 fl oz/½ cup) vegetable oil

600 g (1 lb 5 oz) white onions, thinly sliced

chopped coriander (cilantro), to garnish

For the *laal maas*

3 tbsp ghee

3 dried red Kashmiri chillies

3 bay leaves

2.5 cm (1 in) ginger root, cut into matchsticks

600 ml (20 fl oz/2½ cups) lamb stock or water

salt, to taste

generous handful of bones with marrow (ask your butcher for this)

1 tbsp tomato purée (paste)

½ tsp garam masala

For a smoky flavour (optional)

1 piece of coal

4 cloves

1 tbsp ghee

My travels across India have always given me a chance to explore a diverse variety of regional cooking. A trip to Udaipur in Rajasthan was made totally worth it as I met locals from the region who shared this stellar recipe for a traditional *laal maas*: slow-cooked lamb curry with bone marrow, chillies and spices. I have adapted the recipe based on the availability of ingredients in the UK. I would recommend cooking this curry in ghee for a rich, decadent flavour.

Put the garlic and ginger in a blender with 2 tablespoons of water and blitz to a smooth paste. Put 1 tablespoon of the paste in a large mixing bowl with the lamb and chilli powder (reserving the remaining paste for later). Mix well, then leave to marinate for a few hours, or even overnight. Drain the soaked red chillies, reserving the soaking water, and put the chillies in a blender with 3 tablespoons of the soaking liquid. Blitz to a smooth, fine chilli paste. Set aside.

Heat the oil in a large frying pan (skillet) over a medium heat. Add the onions and fry for 45–50 minutes, stirring often, until evenly brown. Drain and set aside.

To cook the *laal maas*, heat the ghee in a large, heavy-based saucepan over a medium heat. Add the chillies and bay leaves and fry for a few seconds, then add the brown fried onions and stir for a minute. Add the marinated lamb and cook over a medium–high heat for 6–8 minutes, making sure you stir well. Reduce the heat to medium, then add the ginger matchsticks, the reserved garlic and ginger paste and the ground chilli paste, and fry for a couple of minutes. Add the stock or water, season to taste and add the extra bones. Cover and simmer over a low heat for 30 minutes. Add the tomato purée and continue to simmer for a further 40–45 minutes with the lid on, stirring halfway through. Turn off the heat and leave to rest.

To give the dish a smoky flavour, heat the charcoal over a high flame, then put it in a small heatproof bowl, along with the cloves and the ghee. Nestle the bowl in the centre of the pan with the curry, and cover with a lid. Take the lid off after 10 minutes and remove the bowl. Finish the curry with the garam masala and fresh coriander.

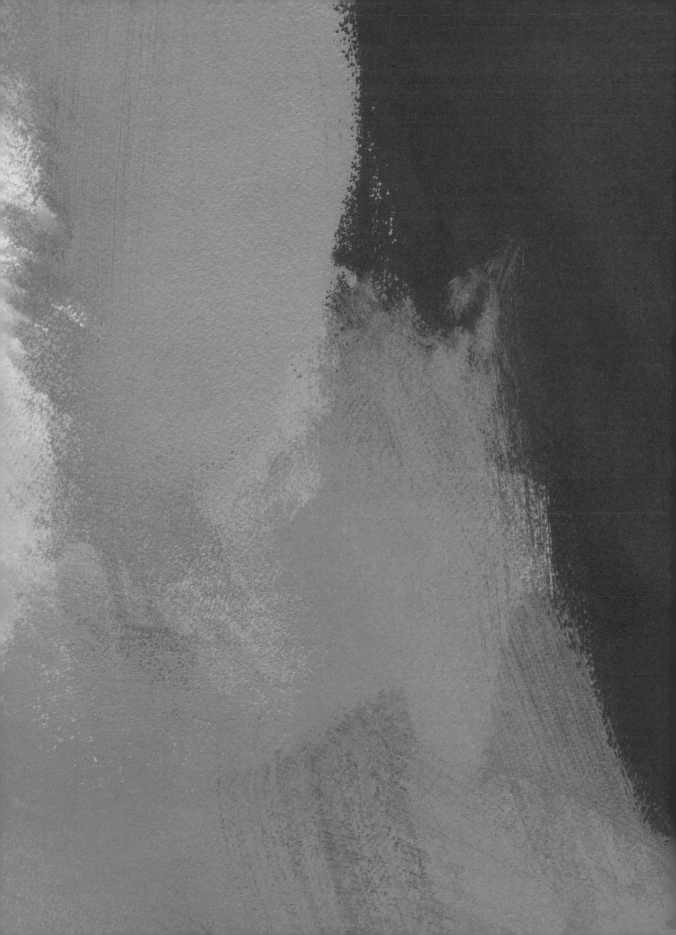

VEGETARIAN CURRIES

With many Indians preferring a vegetarian diet, this chapter is a reflection of the sheer variety of vegetables, spices and cooking techniques used across communities in India. There are plenty of recipes to choose from for a vegetarian or a vegan thali.

Andhra Aubergine, Coconut & Tamarind Stew

SERVES 4

400 g (14 oz) aubergines (eggplants), cut lengthways into batons
6 tbsp vegetable oil
80 g (3 oz) grated fresh or frozen coconut
2 heaped tbsp Greek yoghurt
1 tsp black mustard seeds
1 cm (½ in) cinnamon stick
8 curry leaves
100 g (3½ oz) white onions, thinly sliced
3 garlic cloves, blended to a paste
1 tsp Kashmiri chilli powder or mild chilli powder
1 tsp ground coriander
1 tsp ground turmeric
250 ml (8½ fl oz/1 cup) water
1 tbsp tamarind paste
1 heaped tsp sugar
salt, to taste
chopped coriander (cilantro), to garnish

Coconut, curry leaves and tamarind are the signature flavours of this dish from Andhra, a classic from the region that's hearty, comforting and flavoured with local spices. Coconut thickens the gravy and gives it the required texture.

Preheat the oven to 180°C fan (400°F/gas 6). Put the aubergines in a roasting tray and pour over 4 tablespoons of the oil. Mix well to coat the aubergines, then roast in the oven for 20 minutes. Meanwhile, tip the coconut and yoghurt into a blender and blitz to a coarse, thick paste. Set aside.

Heat the remaining oil in a heavy-based saucepan over a medium heat. Add the mustard seeds, letting them sizzle and crackle in the pan for a few seconds, then add the cinnamon stick and fry for a few seconds. Add the curry leaves and onions and fry for 8–10 minutes over a medium heat until the onions begin to soften and colour, stirring well. Add the garlic paste and fry for 30 seconds.

Reduce the heat to low and add the coconut paste and ground spices. Fry for 4–5 minutes, mixing well, then add the water and tamarind paste, along with the sugar and salt to taste. Bring to a simmer and add the cooked aubergines.

Cover and cook over a low heat for 8 minutes until the gravy coats the aubergines and they are cooked through, stirring halfway through to make sure the curry doesn't stick to the bottom of the pan. Garnish with fresh coriander and serve with chapattis or plain rice.

BEDMI ALOO
Spiced Turmeric & Coriander Potato Curry

SERVES 4

5 cm (2 in) ginger root, roughly chopped
2 green bird's-eye chillies, roughly chopped
2 tbsp ghee
1 tsp cumin seeds
pinch of asafoetida
½ tsp Kashmiri chilli powder
1 tsp ground turmeric
1 tsp ground coriander
1 tbsp tomato purée (paste)
700 g (1 lb 9 oz) new potatoes, peeled and halved
600 ml (20 fl oz/2½ cups) water
pinch of sugar
salt, to taste
1 tsp dried mango powder
chopped coriander (cilantro), to garnish

A delicious way to cook a classic potato curry with cumin, chilli, turmeric and coriander in a light, soupy gravy. This simple-to-cook dish is eaten all across Uttar Pradesh and savoured with puris.

Put the ginger and chillies in a blender and blitz to a coarse paste, then set aside.

Heat the ghee in a heavy-based, non-stick pan over a medium heat. Working quickly, add the cumin seeds and asafoetida to the pan and fry for a few seconds until they sizzle, then add the ginger and chilli paste and fry for a minute.

Add the chilli powder, turmeric and ground coriander, then add the tomato purée and cook for 1 minute, stirring well. Add the potatoes and mix gently for 1–2 minutes, making sure they are coated in the spices. Add the water and sugar, and season to taste.

Bring to the boil, then cover and simmer over a low heat for 30 minutes until the potatoes are cooked through. Crush some of them lightly to thicken the gravy.

Add the mango powder and fresh coriander. Turn off the heat and serve with puris, raita and pickle.

Chickpea & Tomato Curry with Ginger & Dried Mango

SERVES 4

3 tbsp vegetable oil or ghee

pinch of asafoetida

200 g (7 oz) white onions, thinly sliced

6 green cardamom pods, whole

4 garlic cloves, crushed to a coarse paste

5 cm (2 in) ginger root, cut into matchsticks

2 tsp cumin seeds, coarsely crushed

1 tbsp ground coriander

½ tsp Kashmiri chilli powder or mild chilli powder

180 g (6½ oz) tomatoes, roughly chopped

2 x 400 g (14 oz) tins of chickpeas (garbanzos), drained

500 ml (17 fl oz/2 cups) water or vegetable stock

salt, to taste

1 heaped tsp dried mango powder

chopped coriander (cilantro), to garnish

A light, brothy, soupy chickpea curry with cumin, tomato and ginger, plus one of my favourite ingredients, dried mango powder, which lends a lovely sour, tart flavour to the gravy.

Heat the oil in a large saucepan over a medium heat. Add the asafoetida and the onions and fry for 8–10 minutes, stirring well until they begin to soften and change colour. Add the green cardamom and stir for 1 minute, then add the garlic and most of the ginger and fry for 20 seconds, stirring to make sure it doesn't stick to the bottom of the pan.

Add the crushed cumin seeds, ground coriander and chilli powder, and fry for 1 minute. Add the tomatoes and stir well, scraping up any sticky bits from the bottom of the pan. Soften the tomatoes for 4–5 minutes. Add the chickpeas and mix well for 4–5 minutes, making sure they are coated in the spices. Add the water or stock, season to taste, then cover and simmer over a low heat for 20–25 minutes, stirring halfway through.

Once cooked, mash some of the chickpeas with the back of the spoon, then turn off the heat. Add the reserved ginger matchsticks, along with the mango powder and fresh coriander. Serve on your thali with freshly made puris.

Creamy Mushroom & Green Pea Curry

SERVES 4

50 g (2 oz) cashew nuts, soaked in warm water for 30 minutes
4 cm (1½ in) ginger root, roughly chopped
5 garlic cloves, roughly chopped
3 tbsp vegetable oil
200 g (7 oz) onions, finely chopped
½ tsp Kashmiri chilli powder
150 g (5 oz/⅔ cup) Greek yoghurt, whisked
450 ml (15¼ fl oz/scant 2 cups) whole milk
300 g (10½ oz) button mushrooms, halved
pinch of sugar
salt, to taste
150 g (5 oz) frozen green peas, defrosted
2 tbsp chopped coriander (cilantro), to garnish

For the spice powder
5 cloves
1 cm (½ in) cassia bark
5 green cardamom pods, seeds only

North Indian cuisine always has some of the finest vegetarian dishes the country has to offer, taking advantage of the seasonality of ingredients, the wealth of available spices and also the abundance of dairy produce within the region. This mushroom and green pea curry is a perfect example: I have cooked it with a creamy cashew paste and yoghurt, which give a mild flavour alongside the spices. If you are vegan, use a dairy-free yoghurt and milk.

Start by making the spice powder. Roast all the spice powder ingredients in a dry frying pan (skillet) for 1–2 minutes until fragrant. Leave the mixture to cool, then grind to a fine powder and set aside.

Drain the soaked cashew nuts, reserving the liquid. Add the nuts to a blender, along with 3–4 tablespoons of the soaking liquid, and blitz to make a smooth paste. Remove and set aside. In the same blender, blitz the ginger and garlic with 2 tablespoons of water and grind to a smooth paste.

Heat the oil in a heavy-based saucepan over a medium heat. Add the onions and fry for 8–10 minutes, stirring, until they are light brown. Add the garlic and ginger paste and fry for a further 1 minute, stirring well to make sure it doesn't stick to the bottom of the pan. Reduce the heat to low and add the chilli powder. Let it cook for 5 seconds, then add the cashew nut paste and ground spices and stir well for 1 minute.

Keeping the heat on low, add the Greek yoghurt, a little at a time, stirring well to ensure it doesn't split. Fry for 5 minutes until the gravy begins to thicken and the oil begins to separate. Add the milk and stir well, making sure there are no lumps in the mixture. Add the mushrooms, sugar and salt and stir well. Increase the heat to high and bring to the boil, then reduce the heat to low, cover and simmer for 5 minutes.

Add the green peas and fresh coriander. Turn off the heat and keep warm until ready to serve. Serve with your choice of bread or rice.

VEGETARIAN CURRIES

Paneer Koftas in a Creamy Spiced Tomato Curry

MAKES 16 KOFTAS

For the koftas
300 g (10½ oz) potatoes,
  boiled, grated
200 g (7 oz) paneer,
  finely grated
1 tsp ground turmeric
1 tsp ground cardamom
¼ tsp garam masala
2.5 cm (1 in) ginger root,
  finely grated
1 green bird's-eye chilli,
  finely chopped
pinch of salt
2 tbsp finely chopped
  coriander (cilantro) leaves
3 tsp cornflour (cornstarch)
2 tbsp raisins

For the gravy
90 g (3¼ oz) cashew nuts,
  soaked in warm water
  for 30 minutes
6 garlic cloves
2.5 cm (1 in) ginger root,
  roughly chopped
2 green bird's-eye chillies,
  1 roughly chopped and
  1 slit lengthways
150 g (5 oz) white onions,
  roughly chopped
200 g (7 oz) tomatoes,
  roughly chopped
3 tbsp vegetable oil, plus
  extra for deep-frying
6 cloves
2.5 cm (1 in) cinnamon
  stick, halved
2 tbsp tomato purée (paste)
½ tsp Kashmiri chilli powder
200 ml (7 fl oz/1 cup) water
1 tsp sugar
½ tsp garam masala
2 tsp dried mango powder
salt, to taste
chopped coriander
  (cilantro), to garnish

A traditional curry hailing from the north of India, *malai koftas* are vegetarian koftas or croquettes made with spiced potato and paneer steeped in a tomato curry. Every dinner party my mother hosted included this kofta curry, although you can also make the koftas as a crispy snack to serve with a green chutney.

To start the gravy, in a blender, blitz the soaked cashew nuts with about 3 tablespoons of its soaking water, to form a smooth, creamy paste. Remove and set aside. In the same blender, blend the garlic, ginger and chopped chilli with a splash of water to a smooth paste, then remove and set aside. Put the onions in the blender with a splash of water and blend to a smooth paste, then set aside. In the same blender, blitz the tomatoes to a fine purée and set aside.

To make the koftas, mash the grated potatoes in a large bowl. Add all the other kofta ingredients and knead lightly to a smooth dough-like consistency. Cover with cling film (plastic wrap) until ready to fry.

Continue making the gravy. Heat the oil in a heavy-based saucepan over a medium heat. Add the whole spices and fry for a few seconds. Add the slit green chilli, followed by the onion paste, and fry for 5 minutes, stirring well. Add the ginger, garlic and chilli paste and fry for 2 minutes, stirring, then add the blended tomato mixture. Mix well and cook for 6–7 minutes. The gravy will begin to reduce and turn a deeper red colour. Add the chilli powder and the cashew nut paste, stir and cook for a further 2 minutes. Reduce the heat to low, and add the water, then bring to a simmer for 2–3 minutes. Add the remaining gravy ingredients and taste for seasoning. Garnish with fresh coriander, turn off the heat and cover, to keep the curry warm.

To fry the koftas, heat enough oil in a *kadhai* or wok (fill around a third of the pan), on a medium-high heat. Test the oil is hot by dropping a piece of bread into it – if it sizzles and browns in 30 seconds, it is done. Divide the kofta mixture into equal portions, and roll each one into a cylindrical shape. Fry them in batches, 2 or 3 at a time, for 3–4 minutes, or until they go a crispy golden brown. Drain on paper towels.

Add the warm gravy to a serving dish and steep the koftas just before serving, and serve with rice, salad and raita.

Spiced Yoghurt Curry with Fenugreek Dumplings

SERVES 4

For the dumplings (*gatte*)
150 g (5 oz/heaped 1⅓ cups) chickpea (gram) flour
1½ tbsp Greek yoghurt
pinch of ground turmeric
½ tsp Kashmiri chilli powder or mild paprika
pinch of baking powder
salt, to taste
3 tbsp dried fenugreek leaves (*kasoori methi*)
1 tsp grated ginger root
3 tbsp vegetable oil, plus extra for oiling and deep-frying

For the curry
3 heaped tbsp Greek yoghurt
1 heaped tsp ground coriander
½ tsp Kashmiri chilli powder
1 tsp ground turmeric
3 tbsp vegetable oil
½ tsp asafoetida
1 tsp cumin seeds
120 g (4 oz) onions, ground to a paste
½ tsp mango powder
salt, to taste
roughly chopped coriander (cilantro), to garnish

Rajasthanis are renowned for recipes that are full of flavour. These *gatte*, or dumplings, absorb the flavours of chilli, turmeric and fenugreek from the wonderfully spicy sauce. Once fried, the *gatte* can be frozen and can be added to the simmering curry straight from the freezer, until they are warmed through and softened.

In a bowl, mix together all the dumpling ingredients, to form a sticky dough base. Oil your palms and divide the dough into 5 thin cylindrical portions, each one no wider than the width of your finger, as they tend to expand once cooked. Leave the *gatte* to rest for 15 minutes before cooking them.

Bring 1.5 litres (52 fl oz/6¼ cups) water to the boil in large, wide pan, over a high heat. Tip the *gatte* gently into the boiling water, a few at a time, and cook them for 10 minutes. They will start to float once they are nearly done. Remove and set aside to cool slightly. Don't worry if they look a little rough around the edges or break slightly; they will firm up once they are fried. Reserve 650 ml (22 fl oz/2¾ cups) of the water to make the curry. Leave the *gatte* to cool for 10 minutes, then cut them into bite-sized pieces.

To fry the *gatte*, heat enough oil in a *kadhai* or wok (it should fill around a third of the pan), on a medium-high heat. Test the oil is hot enough by dropping a piece of bread into it – if it sizzles and browns in 30 seconds, it is done. Fry the *gatte* in batches for 3–4 minutes, until golden brown. Drain on paper towels and set aside while you make the curry.

To make the curry, whisk the yoghurt with the ground coriander, chilli powder and turmeric and set aside. Heat the oil in a heavy-based saucepan over a medium heat, then add the asafoetida and cumin seeds and let them sizzle for a few seconds. Now tip in the onion paste and fry for a couple of minutes. Take the pan off the heat, add the whisked yoghurt, then put it back over a low heat for 2–3 minutes, stirring continuously to make sure the sauce doesn't split. Add the reserved dumpling water to the pan to form a runny gravy. Bring the curry to a simmer for 5 minutes. Add the *gatte* and

See recipe photo overleaf

Recipe continued opposite >

continue cooking for a further 5 minutes, still over a low heat without a lid, so the *gatte* can soak in all the spiced goodness.

You can leave the *gatte* to soak in the curry for a few hours. If the gravy is quite thick, add a little more water to get it to a lighter consistency. Turn off the heat, add the mango powder, season to taste and garnish with fresh coriander. Serve with fresh rotis or steamed basmati rice.

PALAK SUVA KI SABZI

Garlic, Spinach & Dill Dal

Dill is such an underrated ingredient in Indian cooking, and yet it is used in many dishes all across the subcontinent. Spinach and dill come together perfectly in this spiced lentil curry. I tend to buy large bunches of dill from Asian stores, as the quantities are generous.

Put the chana dal in a saucepan with plenty of water. Bring to the boil and simmer over a medium heat for 45 minutes, stirring often. The chana dal should be tender but still holding its shape. Drain and set aside. Put the ginger, garlic and chillies in a blender with a splash of water and blend to smooth paste, then set aside.

Heat the oil in a large, non-stick saucepan over a medium heat. Add the cumin seeds and asafoetida and fry for a few seconds until they begin to sizzle, then add the ginger, garlic and chilli paste and fry for a few seconds, stirring well. Add the tomatoes and cook for 4 minutes until they begin to soften.

Add the turmeric and coriander, along with the cooked chana dal, and fry for 4–5 minutes. Season to taste and add the spinach and dill, a little at a time. Keep stirring for 3–4 minutes as they begin to wilt. Reduce the heat to low, cover and continue to cook for 5 minutes, stirring halfway through. Turn off the heat and serve with rotis, pickle and *kadhi*.

See recipe photo overleaf

SERVES 4

150 g (5 oz/¾ cup) chana dal
5 cm (2 in) ginger root, roughly chopped
6 garlic cloves, roughly chopped
2 green bird's-eye chillies, roughly chopped
3 tbsp vegetable oil
1 tsp cumin seeds
pinch of asafoetida
100 g (3½ oz) tomatoes, finely chopped
1 tsp ground turmeric
1 tbsp ground coriander
salt, to taste
250 g (9 oz) spinach leaves, washed and finely chopped
100 g (3½ oz) dill fronds, finely chopped

From left to right: Rajasthani Gatte ki Sabzi (page 96);
Palak Suva ki Sabzi (page 97); Bihari Bari Kadhi (page 101)

VEGETARIAN CURRIES

BIHARI BARI KADHI

Gram Flour Dumplings in a Spicy Yoghurt Gravy

MAKES 18–20 *BARI*

For the *bari* (dumplings)
150 g (5 oz/1⅓ cups)
   chickpea (gram) flour
salt, to taste
½ tsp ground turmeric
½ tsp garlic paste
1 tsp ground coriander
½ tsp mild chilli powder
1 tsp carom seeds
180 ml (6½ fl oz/scant
   1 cup) water
1 tsp Eno or fruit salt
vegetable oil, for
   deep-frying

For the *kadhi*
100 g (3½ oz/scant 1 cup)
   chickpea (gram) flour
1 tsp ground turmeric
200 g (7 oz/1⅔ cups)
   Greek yoghurt
400 ml (13 fl oz/generous
   1½ cups) water
½ tsp garlic paste
1 tsp ground coriander
½ tsp mild chilli powder

For the *tadka*
3 tbsp vegetable oil
2 tsp cumin seeds
2 dried red mild chillies
12–14 curry leaves
100 g (3½ oz) white onions,
   finely chopped
salt, to taste
½ tsp garam masala
chopped coriander
   (cilantro), to garnish

The variety of yoghurt-based curries across India is a thing of wonder, and a testament to the versatility of each region. I have been yearning to share this recipe from the regions of Bihar; it is unique, delicious and so full of flavour. *Bari* are dumplings made using chickpea flour and simmered in the spiced yoghurt curry.

In a bowl, mix all the *bari* ingredients, except the water, Eno or fruit salt and oil. Add the water and whisk to form a smooth batter consistency. Add the Eno or fruit salt to the mix and gently stir as the batter begins to thicken. Leave to rest for 10 minutes.

Heat enough oil in a *kadhai* or wok, on a medium-high heat (it should fill around a third of the pan). To check the oil is hot enough, drop a small amount of batter into the oil – it should sizzle and gradually rise to the surface of the oil, and brown in around 30–60 seconds.

When you are ready to start frying, using a couple of tablespoons, add scoops of the batter to the hot oil. Fry the *bari* in batches for 2–3 minutes. You want the exterior to be crispy and golden brown, while the insides are cooked all the way through. Drain on paper towels and keep warm while you cook the remaining batches.

To make the *kadhi*, put the chickpea flour, turmeric and yoghurt in a mixing bowl. Add the water and whisk well, then add the remaining ingredients and stir well. Set aside.

For the *tadka*, heat the oil in a large, non-stick saucepan over a low heat. Add the cumin seeds and chillies and fry until they begin to sizzle, then add the curry leaves and the onions and fry for 5–7 minutes. Add the *kadhi* mix and stir really well. Add an additional 500 ml (17 fl oz/2 cups) water to the saucepan and season to taste. As it cooks it will continue to thicken; simmer over a low heat for 5–7 minutes, stirring continuously. Turn off the heat and add the garam masala and coriander.

Just before serving, add the *bari* to the *kadhi*. Serve with plain rice and pickle on the side.

New Potatoes in Spiced Mint Gravy

SERVES 4

4 tbsp vegetable oil

800 g (1 lb 12 oz) new potatoes, peeled and halved if large

1 heaped tsp coarsely ground cumin seeds

150 g (5 oz) white onions, thinly sliced

3 tbsp Greek yoghurt, whisked

2 tsp ground coriander

½ tsp mild chilli powder

250 ml (8½ fl oz/1 cup) water

salt, to taste

pinch of garam masala

1 tbsp chopped coriander (cilantro), to garnish

1 tbsp chopped fresh mint, to garnish

1 tsp ginger, sliced into matchsticks, to garnish

For the green chutney

50 g (2 oz) cashew nuts

75 g (2½ oz) fresh mint leaves

50 g (2 oz) coriander (cilantro), leaves and stems

5 cm (2 in) ginger root, roughly chopped

1 green bird's-eye chilli

pinch of sugar

150 ml (5 fl oz/scant ⅔ cup) water

The gravy in this recipe coats the crispy potatoes – so good! Hailing from the region of Uttar Pradesh, this Lucknowi dish is full of flavour and surprisingly simple to make. The creamy gravy with the ground mint and coriander is infused with spices and fresh ginger. I have used new potatoes although you can also swap for regular potatoes.

First prepare the green chutney. Add all the chutney ingredients to a blender and blitz to a smooth, fine paste. Set aside.

Heat 3 tablespoons of the oil in a heavy-based, non-stick saucepan or *kadhai* over a medium heat and add the potatoes. Fry for 18–20 minutes, stirring often as they begin to brown and cook. Now put the lid on and cook for a further 7–8 minutes, stirring halfway through.

Transfer the potatoes onto a plate lined with kitchen paper, and then add the remaining tablespoon of oil to the pan, still over a medium heat. Add the coarsely crushed cumin seeds and fry for a few seconds, then add the sliced onions and fry, stirring well, for 8–10 minutes until they begin to brown. Add the green chutney and stir well. Fry for 2–3 minutes until the moisture begins to evaporate.

Take the pan off the heat and add the yoghurt, a little at a time, stirring well, along with the ground coriander and chilli powder. Return the pan to a low heat and simmer for 1 minute. Add the water and continue to simmer for a further 2 minutes, then add the salt, garam masala and fried potatoes. Turn off the heat and garnish with fresh coriander, mint and ginger matchsticks. Serve warm with pulao or naan.

SINDHI KADHI
Soupy Tamarind & Vegetable Curry

SERVES 4

40 g (1½ oz, heaped ⅓ cup)
   chickpea (gram) flour
1 tsp ground turmeric
½ tsp Kashmiri chilli
   powder or mild paprika
4 tbsp vegetable oil
100 g (3½ oz) okra
   (ladies' fingers), topped
   and tailed, then slit
   lengthways
pinch of asafoetida
1 tsp cumin seeds
½ tsp fenugreek seeds
2 green bird's-eye chillies,
   halved lengthways
2.5 cm (1 in) ginger root,
   grated
8–10 curry leaves
700 ml (24 fl oz/scant
   3 cups) water
2 tbsp jaggery or dark soft
   brown sugar
1½ tbsp tamarind paste
250 g (9 oz) potatoes, cut
   into medium chunks then
   boiled
salt, to taste
coriander (cilantro),
   to garnish

A soupy *kadhi*, or gravy, simmered with cumin, ginger, tamarind and chilli makes a tangy, hot, spicy and moreish meal from this chickpea flour base, perfect to enjoy with a bowl of plain rice. I love adding okra and carrots, along with potatoes, which make it a hearty meal, but it can be adapted to use whatever vegetables you have in your kitchen.

In a bowl, mix together the chickpea flour, turmeric and chilli powder and set aside.

Heat 1 tablespoon of the oil in a large saucepan over a medium heat. Add the okra and fry for 20 seconds, stirring to make sure the oil coats all the pieces. Cover and cook for a further 2 minutes. Take the lid off and shake the pan lightly. Transfer the okra to a plate lined with paper towels, then return the pan to a medium heat and add the remaining oil.

Add the asafoetida and cumin seeds and fry for a few seconds, then add the fenugreek seeds. Stir, then add the green chillies and the ginger and fry for 1 minute. Add the curry leaves and reduce the heat to low. Now add the chickpea flour mix and roast for 2 minutes, stirring continuously.

Take the pan off the heat and add the water, a little at a time. Using a whisk, mix well after each addition, to make sure there are no lumps. Put the pan back on the heat and add the jaggery and tamarind paste. Mix well to blend the tamarind with the gravy. Season to taste, then simmer for 5 minutes over a low heat, stirring halfway through, to make sure it does not stick to the bottom of the pan.

Add the okra and the boiled potatoes and simmer for 2 minutes. Garnish with fresh coriander and serve warm with your thali, along with some rice on the side and some crispy accompaniments.

RINGAN BATATA NU SHAAK

Gujarati Aubergine & Potato Curry

SERVES 4

3 tbsp vegetable oil
2 tsp black mustard seeds
1 tsp cumin seeds
pinch of asafoetida
1 dried mild red chilli
5 cm (2 in) ginger root,
  ground to a paste
300 g (10½ oz) potatoes,
  cut into cubes
½ tsp Kashmiri chilli
  powder or mild
  chilli powder
1 tsp ground turmeric
250 g (9 oz) aubergine
  (eggplant), cut into cubes
1 tsp ground cumin
2 tsp ground coriander
200 ml (7 fl oz/scant 1 cup)
  water
90 g (3¼ oz) tomato,
  roughly chopped
1 green bird's-eye chilli, slit
  lengthways (optional)
1 tsp jaggery or light soft
  brown sugar
salt, to taste
chopped coriander
  (cilantro), to garnish

Cooked with cumin, garlic and coriander, this classic is always part of a traditional Gujarati thali – delicious, but so simple and quick to cook!

Heat the oil in a large, heavy-based, non-stick saucepan over a medium heat. Add the mustard seeds and, when they begin to pop, add the cumin seeds and asafoetida and fry for a few more seconds.

Add the dried chilli and the ginger paste and fry for 10 seconds, stirring well, then add the diced potato and fry for a further 2 minutes, stirring well. Add the chilli powder and turmeric and mix well, before adding the aubergine, cumin and ground coriander. Stir to coat the aubergine in the spices then add the water, cover and simmer for 4 minutes over a low heat.

Add the chopped tomato, the chilli, if using, and the jaggery and season to taste. Stir well, then cover and continue to cook over a low heat for 12–14 minutes until the potato has cooked through, stirring halfway through.

Just before you are ready to eat, garnish with fresh coriander and serve warm with chapatti, raita and pickle.

South Indian Vegetable Kurma

SERVES 4

3 tbsp vegetable oil or
  coconut oil
2 tsp black mustard seeds
120 g (4 oz) white onions,
  finely chopped
5 cm (2 in) ginger root,
  finely chopped
2 green bird's-eye chillies,
  slit lengthways
250 g (9 oz) cauliflower, cut
  into small florets
200 g (7 oz) carrots, diced
200 g (7 oz) potatoes,
  peeled and diced
300 ml (10 fl oz/1¼ cups)
  water
150 g (5 oz) green beans,
  trimmed and quartered
salt, to taste
150 g (5 oz) tomatoes,
  finely chopped
300 ml (10 fl oz/1¼ cups)
  coconut milk
1 tsp coarsely crushed
  black pepper
1½ tsp ground fennel
5–7 curry leaves
pinch of ground cinnamon
 chopped coriander
  (cilantro), to garnish

This creamy kurma from Kerala is one of my favourites. Cooked with fennel, coarsely ground pepper and coconut milk, it encompasses all the goodness of southern Indian flavour, and is an ideal recipe for any vegetables you like.

Heat the oil in a heavy-based, non-stick saucepan over a medium heat. Add the mustard seeds and fry for a few seconds until they sputter.

Add the chopped onions and fry for 8 minutes until they soften, then add the ginger and fry for a further 2 minutes. Add the chillies, cauliflower, carrots and potatoes and fry for 2–3 minutes. Next, add the water and bring to the boil, then cover and simmer over a low heat for 5 minutes.

Add the green beans, season to taste and continue cooking for 3 minutes with the lid on. Stir in the tomatoes and cook for 5 minutes, stirring often to make sure the vegetables don't stick to the bottom of the pan. To finish, add the coconut milk, black pepper, fennel and curry leaves and simmer for 5 minutes.

Turn off the heat and garnish with ground cinnamon and fresh coriander. Serve with soft parathas or pulao.

KUMRO CHENCHKI

Bengali Five-Spice Squash

SERVES 4

3 tbsp vegetable oil

2 heaped tsp *panch phoron* (shop-bought or home-made, see page 20)

2 dried mild red chillies, deseeded

5 cm (2 in) ginger root, crushed to a paste

850 g (1 lb 13 oz) squash or pumpkin, peeled and cut into bite-sized chunks

1½ tsp ground turmeric

1 tsp Kashmiri chilli powder or mild chilli powder

2 heaped tsp ground coriander

2 tsp dark soft brown sugar or jaggery

salt, to taste

100 ml (3½ fl oz/scant ½ cup) water

chopped coriander (cilantro), to garnish

Bengali stir-fried squash or pumpkin is cooked with *panch phoron* and sweetened with soft brown sugar or jaggery. This spice mix is used in lots of Bengali recipes. You can also cook this stir-fry with mustard oil for a slightly more pungent flavour.

Heat the oil in a non-stick wok or *kadhai* over a medium heat. Add the *panch phoron* and red chillies, letting them sizzle for a few seconds, then add the ginger paste and fry for a minute, making sure you stir so it does not burn.

Add the chopped squash or pumpkin and stir for 2–3 minutes before adding the powdered spices and sugar or jaggery. Season to taste and stir well, then add the water and bring to a simmer. Reduce the heat to low, cover and cook for 6 minutes. Stir, add a splash more water and continue to cook for a further 10–12 minutes with the lid on. You want the squash to be fully cooked, yet holding its shape.

When you are ready to eat, garnish with fresh coriander and serve with dal, pickles, flatbreads such as *luchi,* or puris.

Spiced Paneer with Tomato & Green Peas

SERVES 4

1 heaped tsp cumin seeds

1 heaped tsp coriander seeds

5 cm (2 in) ginger root, roughly chopped

3 garlic cloves, roughly chopped

200 g (7 oz) tomatoes, roughly chopped

2 heaped tbsp tomato purée (paste)

3 tbsp vegetable oil

250 g (9 oz) white onions, finely chopped

1 heaped tsp ground turmeric

1 tsp Kashmiri chilli powder or mild chilli powder

1 tsp sugar

salt, to taste

350 ml (12¼ fl oz/1½ cups) water

500 g (1 lb 2 oz) paneer, diced into bite-sized pieces

150 g (5 oz) frozen green peas

½ tsp garam masala

handful of chopped coriander (cilantro), to garnish

Travelling through the bustling by-lanes of Old Delhi when I visit India is always a reminder of how popular paneer is. You can spot loads of dairy shops that stock paneer. It is a versatile ingredient, used in Indian vegetarian cooking, and has a mild flavour, which is great as it soaks up all the goodness of the spices. In fact, most street stalls serve fresh paneer simply sprinkled with spices because it is so good.

Paneer cooks really quickly, so if you are making this curry in advance, my tip is to fry the paneer prior to making the gravy. Once fried, soak it in water while you are making the curry, so it stays soft. Add the paneer right at the end, while the gravy is simmering.

In a spice grinder or pestle and mortar, grind the cumin seeds and coriander seeds to a powder and set aside. In a blender, blend the ginger and garlic with a splash of water to form a smooth paste, then remove and set aside. In the same blender, blitz the tomatoes, along with the tomato purée, and set aside.

Heat the oil in a heavy-based non-stick saucepan over a medium heat. Add the onions and fry for 12–14 minutes, stirring well as they begin to change colour, then add the ginger and garlic paste. Fry well for 2 minutes, stirring continuously. Add the ground cumin and coriander seeds, along with the turmeric and chilli powder. Fry for 1 minute, then add a splash of water, stirring to make sure it doesn't stick to the bottom of the pan. Continue cooking out the raw flavour of the spices for a further minute.

Tip in the blended tomatoes and cook for 5–7 minutes, stirring well. At this stage, add the sugar, salt and water. Cover and simmer over a low heat for 5–6 minutes. Add the paneer and continue to simmer for 5 minutes, then add the frozen green peas and the garam masala. Simmer for 2 minutes, then turn off the heat. Garnish with fresh coriander and serve with paratha or pulao and raita.

VEGETARIAN CURRIES

MUTTAI THOKKU
Spiced Egg Curry with Fennel & Chilli

SERVES 4

4 tbsp vegetable oil
2 dried mild red chillies
12–15 curry leaves
500 g (1 lb 2 oz) white onions, finely diced
8 garlic cloves, pounded to a smooth paste
500 g (1 lb 2 oz) tomatoes, finely diced
2 tsp sugar
2 heaped tbsp tomato purée (paste)
1½ tsp Kashmiri chilli powder
1½ tsp ground turmeric
1 tbsp ground coriander
2 tsp ground fennel
300 ml (10 fl oz/1¼ cups) water
salt, to taste
6 eggs, boiled, peeled and halved or roughly chopped
chopped coriander (cilantro), to garnish

I remember making notes for a recipe I cooked in a local home in Chennai a few years back. Handwritten notes without measurements, that frankly always made me wonder if I would ever get the recipe right! The recipe was narrated to me by Rashida Rehman. At the age of 73, she still cooked regularly for her family, and she made this delicious egg curry for me. *Muttai thokku* ('muttai' meaning eggs) is made with a rich tomato gravy base. The balance of tomato with a pinch of sugar and chilli powder is what really makes this dish a stellar addition to any meal. The gravy must be slow-cooked, and even though it takes some time, it's worth it. I try to source good-quality tomatoes for a recipe like this, but if that's tricky, I add tomato purée, as I have done in this recipe, which helps thicken the sauce whilst giving a lovely colour.

Heat the oil in a heavy-based saucepan over a medium heat. Add the dried chillies and half the curry leaves and let them sputter for a few minutes, then add the onions and fry for 25–30 minutes, stirring well to make sure they don't stick to the bottom of the pan.

Add the garlic paste and fry well for 1 minute. Add the tomatoes and continue to cook for 10 minutes. They will begin to soften and go slightly mushy. Add the sugar, along with the tomato purée, and stir well as you fry for 2 minutes. Add the powdered spices and fry for a further 2 minutes. Now add the water and bring to the boil, then reduce the heat to low and simmer for 25 minutes, stirring halfway through.

Season to taste and add the eggs. Continue to simmer for 2–3 minutes. Garnish with fresh coriander and the remaining curry leaves, and serve with paratha or rice.

Kidney Bean Curry with Cardamom, Ginger & Chilli

SERVES 4

2.5 cm (1 in) ginger root
5 garlic cloves
3 tbsp ghee or vegetable oil
4 black cardamom pods, whole
5 cm (2 in) cinnamon stick
130 g (4 oz) white onions, finely chopped
2 heaped tbsp tomato purée (paste)
2 x 400 g (14 oz) tins of red kidney beans, drained and rinsed
2 tsp ginger powder
½ tsp mild chilli powder
pinch of asafoetida
350 ml (12¼ fl oz/1½ cups) water
salt, to taste
pinch of garam masala
chopped coriander (cilantro), to garnish

Ask any Punjabi what is the definition of comfort food and *Rajma Chawal* will be at the top of that list. I have eaten versions of this red kidney bean curry in many thalis across the years so I felt it fell upon me to include a recipe I rely on when I need my comfort food fix! This one includes black cardamom, which lends a wonderful smoky flavour, along with chilli, tomato and garam masala. It's simple to cook as I've opted for tinned kidney beans, although you can always soak and cook with the dried variety too.

First, put the ginger root and garlic cloves into a blender, with a splash of water, and blend to form a smooth paste.

Heat the ghee or oil in a large, heavy-based saucepan over a low heat. Add the black cardamom pods and cinnamon stick, letting them fry for 1 minute. Add the ginger and garlic paste and fry for 30 seconds as the raw flavours cook through.

Increase the heat to medium, add the chopped onions and cook for 14–15 minutes as they soften and go light brown. Stir well, making sure the mixture doesn't stick to the bottom of the pan.

Add the tomato purée and fry for 2 minutes, then add a splash of water and scrape off any sticky bits from the bottom of the pan. Now add the red kidney beans, along with the ginger and chilli powder, and asafoetida. Stir well and fry for 1 minute, then add the water and season to taste.

Cover and cook over a low heat for 17–18 minutes, stirring halfway through. Crush some of the beans with the back of the spoon to thicken the gravy slightly. Finish with the garam masala, garnish with fresh coriander and serve with rice and *papad*.

MOR KEERAI KUZHAMBU
Yoghurt, Spinach & Coconut Curry

2 tbsp vegetable oil
1 tsp black mustard seeds
1 tsp cumin seeds, coarsely crushed
1 tsp fenugreek seeds
260 g (9½ oz) spinach, washed and finely chopped
1 tsp ground turmeric
salt, to taste

For the chilli and coconut-yoghurt paste
300 g (10½ oz/1¼ cups) Greek yoghurt
400 ml (13 fl oz/generous 1½ cups) water
90 g (3¼ oz) grated fresh or frozrn coconut
1 green bird's-eye chilli
2.5 cm (1 in) ginger root

Using ingredients favoured within the Tamil communities – including mustard seeds, fenugreek, grated coconut and chilli – this curry is so good eaten with plain rice!

First make the chilli and coconut-yoghurt paste. Put the yoghurt and water in a large bowl and whisk together until smooth. Put the remaining paste ingredients in a blender with a few spoonfuls of the yoghurt and water mixture, and blend to form a smooth, fine paste. Add the blended chilli and coconut paste to the remaining yoghurt in the bowl, then set aside.

Heat the oil in a heavy-based, non-stick saucepan over a medium heat. Add the mustard seeds, cumin seeds and fenugreek seeds and fry for a few seconds.

Add the spinach and turmeric and fry for 5-7 minutes, stirring well as the spinach wilts. Remove the pan from the heat and pour in the chilli and coconut-yoghurt mixture.

Return the pan to a low heat and simmer for 5–6 minutes, stirring continuously. Season to taste and serve warm with rice, pickle and *papad*.

ANDHRA MUTHAPAPPU

Vegetable, Coconut & Moong Dal

SERVES 4

200 g (7 oz/1 cup) moong dal (husked and halved yellow mung beans)
pinch of salt, plus extra to taste
1 tsp ground turmeric
1.1 litres (37 fl oz/4½ cups) water
3 tbsp vegetable oil or ghee
1 heaped tsp black mustard seeds, coarsely crushed
1 tsp Kashmiri chilli powder or mild chilli powder
1 tbsp ground coriander
250 g (9 oz) carrots, cut into bite-sized pieces
200 g (7 oz) green beans, trimmed and finely chopped
70 g (2¼ oz/ 1 cup) grated fresh or frozen coconut
chopped coriander (cilantro), to garnish

A hearty vegetable and coconut recipe made with moong dal, chilli, mustard seeds and turmeric, this makes a lovely addition to the abundance of flavours and textures that make up a thali, while also being perfect served with plain rice for the ultimate comfort food.

Put the moong dal in a saucepan with a pinch of salt, the turmeric and the water. Bring to the boil, then cook over a medium heat for 30–35 minutes, stirring often to make sure it doesn't stick to the bottom of the pan. Once cooked, turn off the heat and, using a potato masher or stick blender, mash the dal well so it is thick and creamy. Set aside.

Heat the oil in a large saucepan over a medium heat, add the mustard seeds, chilli and ground coriander and fry for a few seconds. Add the carrots and fry for 2–3 minutes, then add the green beans. Stir and cook for a further 2–3 minutes. Add about 3 tablespoons of water, season to taste and simmer over a low heat for 4 minutes until the ingredients are nearly cooked through.

At this stage, add the cooked dal and stir well for another minute, making sure it doesn't stick to the bottom of the pan. Add the grated coconut and fresh coriander and stir. Serve warm with rice.

Broad Bean Curry with Carom Seeds, Jaggery & Tamarind Paste

SERVES 4

3 tbsp vegetable oil
1 tsp carom seeds
pinch of asafoetida
1 tsp Kashmiri chilli powder
   or mild chilli powder
1 tsp ground turmeric
470 g (1 lb 1 oz) tinned or
   jarred butter beans
400 ml (13 fl oz/generous
   1½ cups) water
1 tbsp jaggery or dark
   soft brown sugar
salt, to taste
2 tsp tamarind paste
chopped coriander
   (cilantro), to garnish

Broad beans and sprouts have a huge repertoire particularly in Gujarati food. These are cooked with chilli, turmeric, jaggery and tamarind. Using frozen broad beans, instead of fresh, can speed up the cooking time, although for this recipe, I have opted for tinned butter beans, which lends a rich flavour to the curry and cooks quickly for an easy mid week meal.

Heat the oil in a heavy-based, non-stick saucepan over a medium heat. Add the carom seeds and asafoetida and, when they sizzle, add the chilli and ground turmeric. Add the butter beans and stir well for 2–3 minutes.

Add the water and jaggery and season to taste. Cover and simmer over a low heat for 25 minutes until the beans begin to soften, stirring halfway through.

Add the tamarind paste and stir. Crush some of the beans with the back of the spoon to thicken the curry slightly. Mix well and garnish with fresh coriander.

SEAFOOD CURRIES

Nothing gives me more joy than visiting my local fishmonger's on a Sunday morning and scouring through all the fresh produce. I was brought up in Mumbai, which is on the west coast of India, and we were lucky enough to cook with and eat some of the freshest seafood available. Coming to England meant I had to adjust my recipes to suit local produce, and I was thrilled to find that the fish available here works so well in curries. Most recipes in this chapter use fish cut into steaks, and my fishmonger is always happy to do that for me. This ensures the fish doesn't disintegrate in the curry, while still allowing it to soak up all the spices.

Classic Coconut Fish Curry

SERVES 4

1 tsp ground turmeric
pinch of salt
juice of ½ lime
600 g (1 lb 5 oz) cod, monkfish or sea bass, cut into 3.5cm (1⅓ in) steaks
60 g (2 oz) white onion, roughly chopped
4 cm (1½ in) ginger root, roughly chopped
4 garlic cloves, roughly chopped
2 tbsp vegetable oil
1 tsp black mustard seeds
5 green cardamom pods, whole
2 green chillies, slit lengthways
5-7 curry leaves
100 ml (3½ fl oz/scant ½ cup) water
½ tsp sugar
salt, to taste
400 ml (13 fl oz/generous 1½ cups) coconut milk
1 heaped tsp tamarind paste
½ tsp freshly ground black pepper
2 tbsp chopped coriander (cilantro) leaves, to garnish

A classic fish curry with chilli, pepper, curry leaves, and turmeric simmered in coconut milk, this southern Indian fish curry is a staple in every household because it is so simple to cook. I like to serve it with rice and cucumber salad. Ask your fishmonger to cut the fish into steaks, as they will do it expertly and ensure that the steaks still hold together with the help of a central bone.

Mix ½ tsp of the ground turmeric, with the salt and lime juice and rub into the fish steaks, then set aside. Add the onion, ginger and garlic to a blender and blend to a smooth fine paste with a splash of water. Set aside.

Heat the oil in a heavy-based, non-stick saucepan over a medium heat. Add the mustard seeds and as they begin to sputter, work quickly to add the cardamom pods, green chillies and curry leaves. Add the onion, ginger and garlic paste and fry for 1-2 minutes, then add the remaining ground turmeric, along with the water, sugar and salt. Mix well, then simmer for 1 minute.

Reduce the heat to low, then add the fish steaks and let them cook for a further minute. Add the coconut milk, cover and simmer gently for 4–5 minutes until the fish is moist and cooked through. Give the pan a gentle swirl a couple of times to make sure everything is mixed but the fish pieces don't break up.

Add the tamarind, black pepper and fresh coriander and stir well, simmering for 1 minute. Serve with plain basmati rice and a cucumber salad.

BANGDA MASALA

Crispy Fried Mackerel with Tamarind & Curry Leaves

SERVES 4

2 whole mackerel, gutted, trimmed and cleaned
6 tbsp coarse semolina
2 tbsp rice flour
pinch of salt
vegetable oil, for shallow frying
lemon wedges, to serve

For the masala
2 large garlic cloves, roughly chopped
2.5 cm (1 in) ginger root, roughly chopped
2 tbsp tamarind paste
3 tsp Kashmiri chilli powder
1 tsp ground turmeric
5–6 curry leaves
1 tbsp ground coriander
salt, to taste
2 tbsp vegetable oil

Mackerel is a firm favourite in the west of India, a region renowned for its coastal cooking, and no thali there is complete without a crispy fried piece of *bangda*, smeared with a spiced masala including chilli, turmeric, tamarind paste and garlic, then coated in semolina and pan-fried.

Put all the masala ingredients in a blender with about 3 tablespoons of water and blitz to a smooth paste. Rub the mackerel with the masala and set aside in the fridge for an hour.

Mix the semolina and rice flour together in a bowl and season lightly, as the masala paste already contains salt. Coat the marinated mackerel in the semolina mixture to create a crust.

You can cook the fish in two ways: heat enough oil in a heavy-based frying pan (skillet) over a low–medium heat. Add the fish to the pan and cook for 4–5 minutes on each side. Flip the fish carefully, making sure the crust stays in place. Or, you can lay a piece of baking paper in the frying pan, then add the oil and fry the fish as before. This gives a lovely crusty coating without overcooking the fish.

Serve your fried mackerel on your thali with lemon wedges.

GOAN FISH AMBOTIK
Hot & Sour Fish Curry

650 g (1 lb 7 oz) sea bream
   or haddock, cut into
   steaks with the centre
   bone intact (any white
   fish works well here)
½ tsp ground turmeric
pinch of salt
100 g (3½ oz) tomatoes,
   roughly chopped
2 tbsp tomato purée (paste)
3 tbsp vegetable oil
120 g (4 oz) white onions,
   finely chopped
500 ml (17 fl oz/2 cups)
   water
2 tsp sugar
salt, to taste
½ tsp tamarind paste
chopped coriander
   (cilantro), to garnish

For the chilli paste
1 heaped tsp cumin seeds
1 tbsp coriander seeds
10 dried red Kashmiri
   chillies
4 cloves
6 garlic cloves
1 cm (½ in) ginger root,
   roughly chopped
2 tablespoons malt vinegar

Ambat means 'sour' in the local language, and it's the tamarind paste that adds the sour notes here, so adjust the quantity depending on the quality and strength of your tamarind. The sour flavour in this dish is balanced by the heat of the chillies, while the marriage of ground spices, tamarind and good-quality fish undoubtedly makes this a dish of wonder. Every thali in Goa will have a version of *ambotik* with fish or prawns. Tangy, hot, spicy and sweet: all the flavours sing with each mouthful.

Put the fish in a bowl with the turmeric and salt. Mix well and set aside.

To make the chilli paste, dry-roast the cumin and coriander seeds with the dried chillies in a frying pan (skillet) over a low heat for 6–8 minutes. Stir as they release their aromas and change colour. Turn off the heat and leave to cool, then transfer to a spice grinder with the cloves and blitz to a fine powder.

In a blender, add the garlic, ginger and vinegar and blend, adding about 4 tablespoons of water, a little at a time, until smooth. Remove and set aside. In the same blender, blitz the tomatoes and tomato purée to a smooth paste.

Heat the oil in a heavy-based saucepan over a medium heat. Add the onions and fry for 10–12 minutes until they begin to colour, stirring well. Add the blended tomato and continue to fry for 4 minutes, then add the chilli paste and fry for a further 4–5 minutes, stirring well and making sure the mixture doesn't stick to the bottom of the pan. Add the water and sugar and season to taste.

Reduce the heat to low and simmer for 2–3 minutes, then add the fish, cover and cook for a further 6–7 minutes. Give the pan a swirl so the fish doesn't break up. Add the tamarind paste and stir. Continue cooking for another minute, then turn off the heat and garnish with fresh coriander. Serve the curry on your thali with rotis, *phulkas* or rice.

Spicy Bream Stuffed with Onions, Garlic & Tomatoes

SERVES 4

2 whole sea bream, or any medium flat white fish, scaled and gutted (about 300 g (10½ oz) each)
1 tsp ground turmeric
6 tbsp vegetable oil
juice of ½ lemon
salt, to taste
8 garlic cloves, roughly chopped
5 cm (2 in) ginger root, roughly chopped
450 g (1 lb) white onions, thinly sliced
280 g (10 oz) tomatoes, finely chopped
1 tbsp tomato purée (paste)
1 tsp Kashmiri chilli powder
1 tsp ground coriander
2 tbsp raisins
1 lemon, sliced
handful of chopped coriander (cilantro)

This dish has been in my family for generations. It would usually be cooked with a local fish called pomfret, but I am using sea bream here based on availability, and also because it's a flat fish that's easy to stuff as it has a large cavity. Fried onions, chilli, tomatoes and ground spices with raisins make the stuffing so delicious. You can pan-fry this stuffed fish instead of baking it, if you prefer. This recipe is a perfect addition to a decadent fish thali.

Place the fish on a plate and score the flesh a few times on each side. In a small bowl, mix together the turmeric, 1 tablespoon of the oil, 1 tablespoon of the lemon juice and a pinch of salt. Rub this mixture into the fish, making sure it is fully coated in the spices, then set aside to marinate.

In a blender, blend the garlic and ginger with a splash of water, to form a smooth, fine paste. Set aside.

Heat the remaining oil in a large, non-stick frying pan (skillet) over a medium heat. Add the onions and fry for 25–30 minutes, stirring well, until they begin to soften and change colour. When they are browned, add the garlic and ginger paste and fry for 2–3 minutes, then add the chopped tomatoes and tomato purée and fry for 7–8 minutes, stirring well. Add the chilli powder, ground coriander and raisins and fry for 3–4 minutes. Season to taste then add the remaining lemon juice, along with the coriander. Set aside to cool.

Preheat the oven to 200°C fan (425°F/gas 7). Divide the cooled onion mixture into thirds. Stuff each fish with one third, then place the final third into the base of a baking dish (ensure your dish is large enough to fit two fish inside, comfortably). Cover the base mixture with a layer of lemon slices, then place both stuffed fish on top and roast for 20–25 minutes until the skin goes crispy. Serve as part of your thali with dal and other accompaniments.

Turmeric & Mustard Fish Curry

SERVES 4

550 g (1 lb 4 oz) sea bass, cut into 4 cm (1½ in) thick steaks
1 tsp ground turmeric
pinch of salt, plus extra to taste
4 garlic cloves, roughly chopped
2.5 cm (1 in) ginger root, roughly chopped
3 tbsp vegetable oil
1 tsp nigella seeds
2 dried bay leaves
2 green bird's-eye chillies, pricked lightly with a knife
150 g (5 oz) tomatoes, chopped
1 tbsp ground coriander
270 g (10 oz) potatoes, diced in bite-sized cubes
500 ml (17 fl oz/2 cups) water
1½ tsp English mustard, mixed with a splash of water
½ tsp garam masala
1 tbsp chopped coriander (cilantro), to garnish

Turmeric, mustard, chilli and garam masala combined in this light, soupy fish curry that's perfect for an everyday meal. *Jhol* actually means 'soup' or 'stew' and this is a simple and delicious one. Some families add additional vegetables to the curry, including aubergines, although here, I've opted for chunks of potato to make it a hearty meal. The key to cooking a traditional *macher jhol* is using mustard oil, which I don't always have in my kitchen, so adding a dash of fiery English mustard gives the required pungent flavour.

Put the fish on a plate and sprinkle with half the turmeric and a pinch of salt. Set aside. In a blender, blitz the garlic and ginger together with a splash of water to make a paste.

Heat the oil in a heavy-based saucepan over a medium heat. Add the nigella seeds and bay leaves and fry until they sizzle, then add the green chillies, along with the garlic and ginger paste and fry for 1 minute.

Add the chopped tomatoes and fry for 5–6 minutes, stirring well, then add the remaining turmeric and the ground coriander. Add the potatoes and fry for 2 minutes, then add the water and season to taste. Cover and simmer over a low heat for 20 minutes, stirring occasionally.

Add the fish steaks and stir gently, then cover again and simmer for 3–4 minutes until the fish is cooked through. Add the English mustard and garam masala. Simmer for 1 minute.

Turn off the heat and garnish with fresh coriander. Serve on your Bengali thali (page 213) or simply with plain rice.

SEAFOOD CURRIES

Stir-Fried Ginger & Green Chilli Prawns

SERVES 4

3 tbsp vegetable oil

1 tsp carom seeds

1 heaped tsp coriander seeds, crushed to a coarse powder

3 dried red Kashmiri chillies or any mild dried chillies

180 g (6½ oz) white onions, finely chopped

5 garlic cloves, roughly chopped

150 g (5 oz) tomatoes, thinly sliced

12–15 king prawns, shelled and deveined

2.5 cm (1 in) ginger root, cut into matchsticks

handful of coriander (cilantro), finely chopped

2 green chillies, slit lengthways

salt, to taste

1 tsp lemon juice

Kadhai cooking is an Indian technique where the ingredients are cooked quickly. The key when making dishes in a *kadhai* is not using any water; the tomatoes add the required moisture. This recipe is made with prawns, carom seeds (*ajwain*), crushed garlic, coriander and lemon, and the sweet chunks of prawn are coated in this spiced gravy.

Heat the oil in a large frying pan (skillet) over a medium heat. Add the carom seeds, coriander seeds and chillies and fry for a few seconds.

Add the onions and fry for 8–10 minutes, stirring well, until they begin to soften and change colour. Add the garlic and fry for 20 seconds, then add the tomatoes and continue to cook for 4 minutes until they soften.

Add the prawns and fry for 3 minutes, then add the ginger matchsticks, fresh coriander and green chillies. Season and stir well. Cover and cook for 2 minutes over a low heat.

Turn off the heat, then squeeze over the lemon juice and serve warm with naan and raita or even some plain paratha.

Hot & Sour Prawn Pickle

SERVES 4

8 garlic cloves, roughly
   chopped
5 cm (2 in) ginger root,
   roughly chopped
150 ml (5 fl oz/scant ⅔ cup)
   vegetable oil
260 g (9½ oz) white onions,
   finely chopped
12 curry leaves, roughly
   torn
½ tsp ground turmeric
2 tbsp dark soft brown
   sugar or jaggery
1 tsp salt
660 g (1 lb 7 oz) king
   prawns, shelled and
   roughly chopped (this
   can be done in a food
   processor as well)
2 tsp fish sauce

For the chilli paste
12 dried red Kashmiri
   chillies, soaked in plenty
   of warm water for
   30 minutes
1 tbsp cumin seeds
2 tsp black peppercorns
1 tsp ground turmeric
80 ml (2½ fl oz/scant
   ⅓ cup) malt vinegar

My mother would make jars of her *balchao* recipe for the family. Most times I loved eating it in a simple thali with dal, rice and salad but as spicy pickles go this one is good just on its own, too. I have used king prawns, and chopped them roughly, but you could use small prawns instead. A lot of Goan households also add a small portion of crushed dried prawns, known as *sungta*. This lends a unique umami, salty flavour that can be tricky to replicate. Here, I have used fish sauce, which makes this a flavour bomb!

To make the chilli paste, drain the chillies and add them to a blender, along with the remaining paste ingredients. Blend to a smooth, fine paste, then remove and set aside. Blend the garlic and ginger in the same blender with a splash of water and set aside.

Heat the oil in a large, heavy-based, non-stick saucepan over a medium heat. Add the onions and fry for 20–22 minutes until they begin to change colour and soften.

Add the curry leaves and turmeric, along with the garlic and ginger paste, and fry for 2 minutes. Add the chilli paste and fry for a further 2 minutes. Reduce the heat to low, then add the sugar and salt. Stir well and fry for 1 minute, making sure the sugar has dissolved.

Add the prawns at this stage, then cover and cook for 8–9 minutes, stirring halfway through. Add the fish sauce and stir well. Leave to cool, then decant into steralised jars and refrigerate. It will keep for up to 10 days in the fridge.

You can serve the *balchao* warm or cold – I love it cold, simply with a fresh, white bread roll.

DALS

You may be wondering why there is a whole chapter just for dals. It's because they are such an integral part of a thali: in fact, most homes and restaurants serving thalis will include at least two different varieties of dal. I have written these recipes using lentils that I know will be available in the supermarket. They can also easily swapped with red lentils if you prefer, just adjust the cooking times.

Creamy Dal with Cardamom & Coconut

SERVES 4

1.2 litres (40 fl oz/4¾ cups) water
300 g (10½ oz/1½ cups) chana dal
4 cloves
1 heaped tsp ground turmeric
salt, to taste
1 heaped tsp sugar
2 tbsp ghee or vegetable oil
2 dried bay leaves
1 tsp cumin seeds
2 green bird's-eye chillies, slit lengthways
30 g (1 oz) grated fresh or frozen coconut
20 g (¾ oz) raisins
1 tbsp chopped coriander (cilantro), to garnish

For the ground spice mix
8 green cardamom pods, seeds only
5 cm (2 in) cinnamon stick
3 dried red Kashmiri chillies

One of my favourite lentil curries from the east of India, the flavours in this dish are lovely. The mild, smoky dried chillies in the spice powder mix work well with the chana dal and sweet raisins.

Bring the water to the boil in a large saucepan, over a medium heat, then add the chana dal and return to the boil. Cook for 10–15 minutes, stirring often, and lifting off any foam that forms on the top with a slotted spoon.

Add the cloves, turmeric, salt and sugar, and continue simmering for a further 45 minutes until the dal is soft, stirring frequently to make sure it doesn't stick to the bottom of the pan. Turn off the heat and remove and discard the cloves. Crush the dal lightly with a potato masher.

To make the ground spice mix, put the cardamom seeds, cinnamon and chillies in a spice grinder to make a fine powder. Set aside.

Heat the ghee or oil in a non-stick, heavy-based saucepan over a medium heat. Add the bay leaves and cumin seeds and cook for a few seconds until they sizzle. Now add the green chillies and stir for 2–3 seconds. Add the coconut and fry for 2–3 minutes until it begins to turn light brown, then pour in the cooked chana dal, stirring well.

Bring to the boil, then add the raisins and the spice mix. Simmer over a low heat for 4–5 minutes. Add the fresh coriander and serve warm on your thali with parathas, flatbreads such as *luchis*, or steamed rice.

GOAN DALICHA RAS

Spicy Turmeric Dal
with Sichuan Pepper

SERVES 4

200 g (7 oz/scant 1 cup)
  toor dal
1 litre (34 fl oz/4 cups)
  water
10–12 Sichuan
  peppercorns, coarsely
  crushed (halve this if you
  prefer the dish less spicy)
pinch of sugar
salt, to taste

For the coconut paste
100 g (3½ oz) grated fresh
  or frozen coconut
½ tsp ground turmeric
1 tsp mild chilli powder
2 tsp tamarind paste
150 ml (5 fl oz/scant ⅔ cup)
  water

A coconut and lentil curry spiced with Sichuan pepper, turmeric and fresh coconut. In India they use a spice known as *tirphal*, which grows locally in the region of Maharashtra and Karnataka. The flavour is tangy, with a warm heat. Here, I have swapped it for Sichuan pepper, which is readily available, and added some tamarind for the required sour note.

Put the toor dal and water in a large saucepan, over a medium heat and bring to the boil, then simmer for 45–50 minutes until soft, stirring a few times while it's cooking. Turn off the heat, cover and leave to cool slightly.

To make the coconut paste, put the coconut, turmeric, chilli powder and tamarind paste in a blender. Add the water and blend to a smooth, fine paste. Set aside.

Using a stick blender or potato masher, blend the dal to a smooth mix. Heat the dal over a low heat, stirring in the coconut paste and adding a little more water if it's too thick.

Add the Sichuan pepper and sugar and season to taste. Simmer for 7–10 minutes, stirring continuously. Turn off the heat and serve warm with plain rice.

Spiced Garlic & Tomato Dal

SERVES 4

250 g (9 oz/heaped 1 cup) toor dal
1.2 litres (40 fl oz/4¾ cups) water
1 tsp ground turmeric
3 tbsp ghee or butter
pinch of asafoetida
1 tsp coarsely crushed cumin seeds
8–10 curry leaves
70 g (2½ oz) white onion, finely chopped
3 garlic cloves, thinly sliced
2.5 cm (1 in) ginger root, chopped
1 green bird's-eye chilli, finely chopped
¼ tsp mild chilli powder
200 g (7 oz) tomatoes, roughly chopped
salt, to taste

This spiced garlic and tomato dal is a staple in every home across the Andhra region. Ghee lends flavour to dals, and this recipe is no exception. You can use toor dal or red lentils: just adjust the cooking time for red lentils, as they cook much more quickly.

Put the toor dal, water and turmeric in a heavy-based saucepan over a medium heat. Bring to the boil, then reduce the heat and simmer gently for 50 minutes until the dal starts to get mushy, stirring regularly to make sure it doesn't stick to the bottom of the pan. Turn off the heat and mash the dal with a potato masher or stick blender to thicken it, then cover and set aside.

Heat the ghee or butter in a heavy-based saucepan over a medium heat, then add the asafoetida, crushed cumin seeds and curry leaves and fry for a few seconds until they sizzle. Add the onion and fry for 12–15 minutes until it begins to soften and change colour.

Add the garlic and ginger, stir well, and fry for 2 minutes. Stir in the chilli and chilli powder, then add the tomatoes and cook for 5 minutes until they begin to soften.

Stir, then add the mixture to the dal. Stir again, season to taste and serve with rice.

RAJASTHANI PALAK DAL
Garlic-Spiced Spinach & Lentil Dal

SERVES 4

250 g (9 oz/scant 1⅓ cups) moong dal, (husked and halved yellow mung beans)

900 ml (30 fl oz/3¾ cups) water

1 tsp ground turmeric

3 tbsp ghee or sunflower oil

2 tsp black mustard seeds

½ tsp cumin seeds

5 garlic cloves, roughly chopped

1 green bird's-eye chilli, slit lengthways

100 g (3½ oz) spinach, washed and chopped

salt, to taste

juice of 1 lemon

A humble dal can make any day brighter! And I do mean that, given I have eaten a good few varieties of them. This creamy dal from the north-west of India is lightly spiced with cumin, turmeric and garlic, with the addition of fresh spinach.

Put the lentils, water and turmeric in a heavy-based saucepan, over a medium heat. Bring to the boil, then reduce the heat to low, half cover and simmer for 30 minutes until the dal starts to get mushy, stirring a few times while it's cooking. Turn off the heat, mash lightly with a potato masher and set aside.

Heat the ghee or oil In a heavy-based saucepan over a medium heat. Add the mustard and cumin seeds and fry for a few seconds until they begin to sputter. Add the garlic and chilli and fry for a few seconds, moving them around in the pan to make sure they don't burn. Reduce the heat to low, then add the cooked lentils, a little at a time, and fry for a couple of minutes.

Season to taste, add an additional 300 ml (10 fl oz/4 cups) of water. Cover and simmer over a low heat for 4 minutes. Add the spinach and continue to simmer for a further 4 minutes, with the lid on. Add the lemon juice and stir.

Turn off the heat and serve warm on your thali. This can be eaten with *phulkas* or rice.

Garlic & Cumin Dal with Tomato, Chilli & Coriander

SERVES 4

250 g (9 oz/1¼ cups)
  chana dal
1 litre (34 fl oz/4 cups)
  water
1 tsp ground turmeric

For the *tadka*
3 tbsp vegetable oil
1 tsp cumin seeds
110 g (3¾ oz) white onions,
  thinly sliced
4 garlic cloves, thinly sliced
1 tsp fennel seeds, coarsely
  crushed
½ tsp Kashmiri chilli
  powder or mild chilli
  powder
1 tsp ground coriander
90 g (3¼ oz) tomato, finely
  chopped
2.5 cm (1 in) ginger root,
  sliced into matchsticks
salt, to taste
chopped coriander
  (cilantro), to garnish

Google will bring up loads of variations on how to make this. I've opted for this recipe because it's one that was shared by my family friend from Delhi, and no matter how many other versions I've tried, this is the one I keep coming back to.

Put the dal, water and turmeric in a large saucepan, over a medium heat. Bring to the boil, then simmer uncovered for 1¼ hours, until the dal is soft, stirring every few minutes to make sure the dal doesn't stick to the bottom of the pan. Mash lightly with a potato masher, then turn off the heat and set aside.

To make the *tadka*, heat the oil in a frying pan (skillet) over a medium heat. Add the cumin seeds, then after a few seconds, add the onions and fry for 8 minutes, stirring well so that they brown evenly. Add the garlic and fry for a further minute, then add the crushed fennel seeds, chilli powder and ground coriander and stir well. Add the tomato and fry for 2–3 minutes until soft, then add the ginger and fry for a further 1 minute.

Pour the *tadka* mix over the cooked dal. Add enough boiling water to thin out the dal; about 80–100 ml (3 fl oz/⅓ cup–7 fl oz/scant ½ cup). Simmer for a couple of minutes to heat through, season to taste and garnish with fresh coriander. Serve warm with roti or rice.

Sweet & Spicy Dal with Chillies & Peanut

SERVES 4

1 heaped tbsp skinless raw peanuts
200 g (7 oz/scant 1 cup) toor dal
1.2 litres (40 fl oz/4¾ cups) water
120 g (4 oz) tomatoes, roughly chopped
1 tsp ground turmeric
3 tbsp ghee
1 tsp black mustard seeds
pinch of asafoetida
2 dried red Kashmiri chillies or any dried mild chillies
7–8 curry leaves
1 tsp Kashmiri chilli powder or mild chilli powder
2 tbsp ground jaggery or brown sugar
salt, to taste
juice of 1 lemon
chopped coriander (cilantro), to garnish

Cooked with jaggery, chilli, turmeric and peanuts, this dal is soupy, tangy and a must on every thali. Adjust the jaggery based on the grade and quality, as some varieties can be sweeter than others.

Put the peanuts in a bowl, cover with hot water and leave to soak while you cook the dal.

Put the dal, water, tomatoes and turmeric in a large saucepan, over a medium heat. Bring to the boil, then reduce the heat to low and simmer for 1¼ hours until the dal is thick and soft, stirring a few times as it cooks to make sure it is not sticking to the pan. Turn off the heat and mash with a potato masher, or use a stick blender to coarsely crush the dal and thicken it slightly. Set aside.

Heat the ghee in a frying pan (skillet) over a medium heat. Add the mustard seeds and asafoetida and fry for a few seconds until they sputter, then add the dried chillies and stir well. Turn off the heat and quickly stir in the curry leaves and chilli powder. Pour this mixture over the warm dal and stir well, then drain the peanuts.

Put the dal back over a low heat, then add the peanuts and jaggery and season to taste. Simmer for 5 minutes until the jaggery has dissolved, stirring to make sure the dal doesn't stick to the bottom of the pan. Turn off the heat, add the lemon juice and garnish with fresh coriander. Serve in your Gujarati thali with roti or rice.

SNACKS

If there is one thing Indians really love, it's definitely an afternoon snack! There are plenty to choose from here, and my favourite is the *Andhra Masala Vadai* (page 155) served with warm chai. But these snacks also work really well as part of a thali, bringing different textures and flavours to the overall meal. Snacks cooked for thalis are often made with leftover veg, so feel free to swap in any spare veg you might have in some of these recipes.

Steamed, Spicy Coriander & Coconut Cakes

SERVES 4

100 g (3½ oz) coriander (cilantro) leaves

85 g (3 oz/¾ cup) chickpea (gram) flour

35 g (1¼ oz/scant ¼ cup) rice flour

3 tbsp vegetable oil, plus extra for greasing and shallow-frying

2 tbsp grated fresh or frozen coconut

½ tsp cumin seeds

1 tsp sesame seeds

1 green bird's-eye chilli, finely chopped

½ tsp ground turmeric

¼ tsp mild chilli powder

salt, to taste

Kothimbir is coriander, and this is a traditional recipe for a savoury cake from the Maharashtrian community, made with chickpea flour, coriander and coconut.

Pat the coriander with a paper towel to remove any excess moisture. You want it to be as dry as possible. Finely chop and place in a mixing bowl with the chickpea flour, rice flour and half of the oil. Add the grated coconut, cumin seeds, sesame seeds, green chilli, turmeric and chilli powder, and season to taste. Mix well so that the coriander leaves are coated in the spices. Add about 3 tablespoons of water, a little at a time, and knead the ingredients together to create a dough-like consistency. Add the remaining 1½ tablespoons of oil and knead lightly, coating the dough with the oil.

Set up a steamer and oil the steaming bowl. Divide the dough in half and shape each piece into a cylinder shape no more than 5 cm (2 in) thick. Place in the oiled bowl, making sure there is enough room for the *vade* to expand as they steam. Steam for 20–25 minutes over a medium heat. Leave to cool slightly.

If you don't have a steamer, stand the steaming bowl on a trivet in a large saucepan and fill the saucepan with boiling water to the level of the trivet. Cover and steam as above. Remove the *vade* from the steamer and cut into slices 2-cm (¾-in) thick.

Heat a frying pan (skillet) over a medium heat and add enough oil for shallow-frying. Once the oil is hot, fry the *kothimbir vade* in batches, cooking for 2–3 minutes on each side until they turn golden brown and crispy. Drain on paper towels, while you cook the remaining *vade*, adding more oil as necessary. Serve as part of your thali with some chutney.

GUJARATI MOONG DAL DHOKLA
Steamed Lentil Cake with Ginger & Curry Leaves

SERVES 4

250 g (9 oz/1⅓ cups) green moong dal, (mung beans with skin on)
2.5 cm (1 in) ginger root, roughly chopped
1 green bird's-eye chilli, roughly chopped
180 ml (6 fl oz/¾ cup) water
1 tbsp finely chopped coriander (cilantro) leaves
1 tbsp vegetable oil
juice of ½ lime
salt, to taste
1½ tsp Eno or fruit salt
chopped coriander (cilantro), to garnish
grated fresh or frozen coconut, to garnish

For the *tadka*
2 tbsp vegetable oil
1 tsp black mustard seeds
1 tsp sesame seeds
½ tsp asafoetida
6–8 curry leaves
1 tbsp sugar

This savoury steamed cake is made with ground lentils and flavoured with curry leaves, chilli, ginger and mustard seeds.

Soak the moong dal in a large bowl in plenty of water for 6–7 hours, or preferably overnight.

Pound the ginger and chilli in a pestle and mortar to make a coarse paste. Drain the dal, put it in a blender with the 180 ml (6 fl oz/¾ cup) of water and blend to a smooth, fine paste. Transfer to a mixing bowl and add the ginger and chilli paste, coriander leaves, oil, lime juice and salt. Mix the batter well and set aside.

Set up the steamer and oil and line a round 10–20 cm (7–8 in) cake tin (pan) with baking parchment. Add the Eno or fruit salt to the prepared batter, stirring to make sure it is evenly mixed in. Spoon the mixture into the prepared tin, then steam for 18–20 minutes over a medium heat. If you don't have a steamer, place the baking tin on a trivet in a large saucepan, and fill the saucepan with boiling water to the level of the trivet. Cover and steam as above, topping up with boiling water as necessary. Turn off the heat and let it rest until cool enough to handle. Remove the tin from the steamer, run a knife around the edge to loosen the *dhokla* and carefully turn it out onto a plate. Using a cocktail stick (toothpick), prick a few holes across the surface. Set aside to cool, slightly.

To make the *tadka*, heat the oil in a frying pan (skillet) over a medium heat. Add the mustard seeds and sesame seeds and fry for a few seconds until they sputter, then add the asafoetida and fry for a few seconds more. Turn off the heat and add the curry leaves, sugar and about 3 tablespoons of water, mixing well to make sure the sugar dissolves completely. Spread this mix evenly over the warm *dhokla*. The mixture will seep through the *dhokla* and add moisture and flavour.

Garnish with fresh coriander and grated coconut. Serve warm on your thali with green chutney.

250 g (9 oz/1¼ cups)
  chana dal
2 green bird's-eye chillies
12 curry leaves
5 cm (2 in) ginger root,
  roughly chopped
60 g (2 oz) white onion,
  finely chopped
½ tsp asafoetida
salt, to taste
vegetable oil, for
  deep-frying

ANDHRA MASALA VADAI

Crispy Fried Lentil Patties

These crisp, fried little patties are served with a chutney and are delicious as part of a thali, or can even be served as a snack with chai.

Soak the chana dal in water for 2 hours. In a pestle and mortar, crush the green chillies, curry leaves and ginger to a coarse paste. Set aside.

Drain the dal and transfer to a blender. Blend to a coarse, thick texture; don't worry if there are a few whole pieces of dal. Add 1 tablespoon of water while grinding only if needed. The mix should be fairly thick and coarse.

Tip the ground dal into a mixing bowl and add the chilli paste, onion and asafoetida. Season to taste and mix well, then divide into 12 portions, to make your *vadai*.

Heat enough oil for deep-frying in a wok or *kadhai* (about a third of the way up the pan), and line a large bowl or plate with paper towels. Test the oil is hot enough by dropping a small square of bread into the oil. If it sizzles and browns in 30 seconds, then the oil is ready.

Once the oil is hot, add the *vadai* in batches a few at a time, and fry for 5–7 minutes until they are golden and crisp. Drain on paper towels while you cook the remaining batches, then serve warm, with any chutney of your choice.

Sweet Potato Cakes with Ginger, Chilli & Cumin seeds

SERVES 4 AS A MAIN

500 g (1 lb 2 oz) sweet
  potatoes
200 g (7 oz) floury white
  potatoes, such as Desiree
  or Rooster
5 cm (2 in) ginger root,
  coarsely grated
2 green bird's-eye chillies,
  finely chopped
handful of coriander
  (cilantro) leaves, finely
  chopped
¼ tsp mild chilli powder
1½ tsp cumin seeds,
  coarsely ground
1 heaped tsp chaat masala
salt, to taste
2 tbsp cornflour
  (cornstarch)
200 g (7 oz/2 cups) dried
  breadcrumbs, for coating
vegetable oil, for shallow-
  frying

Traditionally cooked in Indian households as a snack, this *tikki* – or potato cake – is packed with nutritional value. This recipe make 10 medium cake-patties, although you can make them into even smaller patties to serve as part of your thali, with a helping of fresh green mint chutney.

Preheat the oven to 200°C fan (425°F/gas 7). Prick the sweet potatoes all over with a fork and roast on a baking tray for 40 minutes until soft. Leave to cool completely. Once cool, scoop the flesh out into a large bowl. Meanwhile, boil the potatoes for 35–40 minutes until tender. Cool slightly and peel.

Add the cooked, peeled potatoes to the bowl with the sweet potato flesh and mash together, along with the ginger, green chilli, fresh coriander and ground spices. Season to taste and mix well. Add the cornflour. Divide into 8–10 portions and coat with the breadcrumbs, pressing them in lightly. Refrigerate for 20 minutes.

Heat enough oil for shallow-frying in a non-stick frying pan (skillet) over a medium heat. Once the oil is hot, add the potato cakes in batches of 2 or 3, and fry for 3–4 minutes on each side until light brown with a crumbly crisp coating.

Drain on paper towels while you cook the remaining cakes, adding more oil as necessary. Serve warm with a fresh green mint chutney.

Tandoori Paneer with Pickling Spices, Chilli & Yoghurt

SERVES 4

500 g (1 lb 2 oz) paneer, cut into bite-sized pieces
250 g (9 oz) green peppers, cut into cubes
melted butter, to baste
chaat masala, to garnish

For the marinade
6–7 garlic cloves, roughly chopped
2.5 cm (1 in) ginger root, roughly chopped
1 tbsp coriander seeds
1 heaped tsp nigella seeds
5 tbsp Greek yoghurt
1 tsp ground turmeric
½ tsp garam masala
2 tsp shop-bought Indian green chilli pickle, gravy and oil only
salt, to taste

Charred paneer skewers coated in a marinade made with coarsely crushed spices, turmeric and creamy thick yoghurt. The colours and vibrance of this tikka are perfect for any thali. You'll need some wooden or metal skewers for this dish. Any shop-bought green chilli pickle will be good for the marinade.

If you are using wooden skewers, soak them in water while you make the marinade; it will make them less likely to char.

Start by making the marinade. Blend the garlic and ginger in a small blender to a smooth, fine paste, adding a little bit of water. Set aside. In a pestle and mortar, crush the coriander seeds and nigella seeds to a coarse powder, then set aside.

Put the yoghurt in a large bowl with the turmeric, garam masala and the shop-bought chilli pickle gravy and oil. Add the garlic and ginger paste and the ground coriander and nigella seeds. Season to taste and mix well. Now add the paneer cubes and the peppers and coat the pieces well in the marinade. Leave to marinate for at least 1 hour.

When you are ready to cook, heat the grill (broiler) to medium and place a wire rack over a baking tray. Thread the paneer and peppers onto the skewers and place on the rack. Grill for 3–4 minutes until the paneer softens and begins to colour slightly. Turn the skewers, baste with butter and grill for a further 4 minutes. Carefully, take the paneer and pepper pieces off the skewers, put them on a serving plate and sprinkle over the chaat masala. Serve warm with flatbread and fresh mint chutney.

BENGALI BEETROOT CHOP

Crispy Fried Beetroot & Potato Cutlets

SERVES 4

2 tbsp vegetable oil, plus extra for deep-frying
1 heaped tsp cumin seeds
2 green bird's-eye chillies, finely chopped
5 cm (2 in) ginger root, coarsely grated
130 g (4 oz) carrots, coarsely grated
300 g (10½ oz) cooked beetroot, coarsely grated
1 heaped tsp raisins
1 tbsp finely chopped coriander (cilantro)
300 g (10½ oz) boiled potatoes, coarsely grated
1 tsp chaat masala
½ tsp dried mango powder
½ tsp Kashmiri chilli powder or mild chilli powder
salt to taste
2 tbsp dried breadcrumbs

For the coating
4 tbsp cornflour (cornstarch)
70 ml (2½ fl oz/scant ⅓ cup) water
about 150 g (5 oz/1½ cups) dried breadcrumbs, for coating

A classic from the east of India, these tasty cutlets are flavoured with ginger, coriander and chaat masala. I love the addition of raisins. Crispy, spicy and sweet, they make a delicious and unusual snack for your thali.

Heat the oil in a large frying pan (skillet) over a medium heat. Add the cumin seeds and, as they begin to sizzle, add the chillies and ginger and fry for 1 minute. Add the grated carrots and cook for 3–4 minutes. Add the beetroot, mix well, then add the raisins and chopped coriander and mix again. Turn off the heat and leave the mixture to cool.

Put the cooled beetroot mixture in a large mixing bowl and add the potatoes. Add the chaat masala, mango powder and chilli powder, and season to taste. Mix well, and stir in the breadcrumbs. Divide the mixture into 12 portions and shape into rounds or ovals (like shown). Refrigerate for around 20 minutes to firm up.

Heat enough oil for deep-frying in a wok or *kadhai* (about a third of the way up the pan), and line a large bowl or plate with paper towels. Test the oil is hot enough by dropping a small square of bread into the oil. If it sizzles and browns in 30 seconds, then the oil is ready.

Mix the cornflour with the water in a shallow bowl until smooth. Place the breadcrumbs in a separate bowl. Roll one cutlet in the cornflour mixture, then in the breadcrumbs, and then fry in the hot oil for 3–4 minutes until golden brown and crisp. Drain on paper towels while you coat the remaining cutlets and cook them in the same way, one at a time. Serve on your thali with green chutney.

BREADS & RICE

Wholemeal breads or puris, along with a portion of rice, form the backbone of the thali platter. Some days, after a portion of *phulkas*, I also love to devour *khichdi*, and the recipe on page 174 is my go-to: cracked wheat and moong dal cooked in ghee, with spices and vegetables. There's nothing better.

Wholemeal Flatbreads

MAKES ABOUT 16 *PHULKAS*

250 g (9 oz/2 cups) chapatti
flour (*atta*), plus extra for
dusting
2 tbsp ghee, plus extra
to serve
pinch of salt
160–170 ml (5½–6 fl oz/
about ¾ cup) water

Phulkas are softer, smaller version of a classic
Indian chapatti, I'm sharing my way of cooking
these much-needed breads for a thali.

Put the flour in a mixing bowl with the ghee and salt. Now add
the water a little at a time, mixing with a spoon or your fingers
until it starts to come together. Knead well, to form a smooth
dough. Cover the bowl with cling film (plastic wrap) and leave
to rest for 20 minutes.

Divide the dough into 12 equal-sized balls. Flatten each ball
and dust with a little flour. Using a rolling pin, roll out each
one as thinly as possible to around 12.5 cm (5 in) in diameter.

Heat a griddle pan or frying pan (skillet) over a medium
heat, until hot. Add one of the rolled *phulkas* and cook for
30 seconds, then turn it on the other side and cook for a
further minute. As it begins to puff up, turn and cook the first
side again for a further 30 seconds, pressing lightly with the
back of a spatula.

Remove from the heat and spread over the ghee. Cover with
a clean tea towel or paper towel, and keep warm while you
make the rest.

BREADS & RICE

Deep-Fried Bread with Wholemeal Flour

MAKES ABOUT 25 PURIS

250 g (9 oz/2 cups)
  wholemeal flour or sifted
  chapatti flour (*atta*)
pinch of salt
3 tbsp vegetable oil, plus
  extra for rolling and
  frying
180 ml (6 fl oz/¾ cup) water

Crispy fried bread – the perfect accompaniment
to scoop up gravies and vegetable dishes in a thali.
They are small, so you can eat plenty!

Put the sifted flour, salt and vegetable oil in a bowl. Roughly
mix with a spoon. Now gradually mix in the water, a little at
a time, to help bring the dough together. Using your fingers,
knead the dough into a ball until smooth and pliable. If the
dough is too sticky, add a bit more flour, and if it is too dry,
add a touch more water. You should end up with a smooth but
firm/stiff dough. Cover with cling film (plastic wrap) and leave
to rest for 15 minutes or so.

Knead the dough once again and divide into equal-sized balls.
Flatten each ball and rub with a little oil, then roll them out into
8 cm (3¼ in) discs (not too thin otherwise they won't puff up).

Heat enough oil in a *kadhai* or wok for deep-frying (about a
third of the way up the pan), and line a large bowl with paper
towels. Test the oil is hot enough by dropping a small square
of bread into the oil. If it sizzles and browns in 30 seconds,
then the oil is ready.

Once the oil is hot, carefully place in the first puri and deep-fry:
it will sink to the bottom, then rise up again. Using a slotted
spoon, press down lightly on the puri until it begins to puff up,
then turn it over and cook for 2–3 seconds on the other side.
It should be lightly golden in colour, but not too dark.

Lift the puri out and place in the paper towel lined bowl to
drain, whilst you make the rest. Serve them warm.

AJWAIN PARATHA

Layered Flatbread with Carom Seeds

MAKES AROUND 8 PARATHAS

250 g (9 oz/2 cups) chapatti
flour (*atta*), plus extra
for dusting
1½ tsp carom seeds
3 tbsp vegetable oil
pinch of salt
170 ml (6 fl oz/¾ cup) water
melted butter or ghee,
for layering and frying

Carom seeds aren't used often in recipes, but they aid digestion and have a lovely pungent flavour. These breads are perfect to accompany a thali.

Place the flour and carom seeds in a mixing bowl with the oil and salt. Add the water, a little at a time, mixing with a spoon or your fingers until it starts to come together. Knead well to form a smooth dough. Cover the bowl tightly and leave to rest for 20 minutes.

Divide the dough into about 8 equal portions and form each one into a ball shape. Using your rolling pin, roll out each dough ball into a 17 cm (7 in) diameter circle. Spread a little melted butter over one of the dough circles and sprinkle with a little extra flour. Fold in half and spread over a bit more butter followed by a bit more flour, then fold into a quarter again. Dust with a little flour and roll out to a circle, about 20 cm (8 in) diameter.

Heat a griddle pan or frying pan (skillet) over a medium heat. Once hot, add one of the parathas and fry for 1 minute as it puffs up and browns slightly. Turn it over and fry for a further minute on the other side, until there are brown speckles across the paratha. Drizzle ½ tsp melted butter over the top and flip it over once more, adding more butter to this side and cooking for a further 5–6 seconds.

Cover the paratha with a clean tea towel, and keep warm while you make the rest. Serve for breakfast with pickle, or alongside your favourite curry.

TAMARIND RICE
Stir-Fried Rice with Tamarind & Crushed Peanuts

SERVES 4

2 tbsp vegetable oil
1 tsp black mustard seeds
pinch of asafoetida
2 dried mild red chillies
1 tbsp roasted peanuts,
    lightly crushed
¼ tsp Kashmiri chilli
    powder or mild chilli
    powder
8–10 curry leaves
3 tsp tamarind paste mixed
    with 3 tbsp water
2 tsp light soft brown sugar
    or jaggery
350 g (12 oz/1¾ cups)
    basmati rice, cooked and
    cooled
salt to taste

Also known as *puliyodharai*, this southern Indian favourite is plain rice flavoured with tamarind, dried red chillies, curry leaves and crushed peanuts. A pinch of jaggery to balance the flavours and this rice dish is a must on every thali. The strength of tamarind can vary, so reduce or increase the quantity based on how tangy or sharp your paste is. Tamarind rice needs a slight tang to it, and the rice soaks up the flavours well.

Heat the oil over a medium heat. Add the mustard seeds, asafoetida, dried chillies and roasted peanuts and fry for 1 minute.

Add the chilli powder, curry leaves, tamarind paste and sugar and stir well. Turn off the heat. Add the cooked rice, making sure you mix everything together well.

Season to taste, and serve warm.

Vegetable Fried Rice with Ginger & Turmeric

SERVES 4

3 garlic cloves, roughly chopped

2.5 cm (1 in) ginger root, roughly chopped

3 tbsp vegetable oil

1 tsp cumin seeds

2.5 cm (1 in) cinnamon stick

2 dried bay leaves

2 black cardamom pods, whole

5 cloves

140 g (4¾ oz) white onions, finely chopped

2 green bird's-eye chillies, slit lengthways

350 g (12 oz) mixed frozen vegetables (cauliflower, green peas, green beans and carrots)

1 tsp ground turmeric

salt, to taste

350 g (12 oz/1¾ cups) basmati rice, cooked and cooled

½ tsp garam masala

chopped coriander (cilantro), to garnish

I make this pulao when I have friends over. It's definitely one that veggies love, and it is versatile enough to accompany an array of curries. I'm using frozen vegetables for convenience, although you can swap for fresh if you prefer: just make sure to adjust the cooking times.

Crush the garlic and ginger in a pestle and mortar and set aside while you make the pulao.

Heat the oil in a heavy-based, non-stick frying pan (skillet) over a medium heat. Add the cumin seeds, cinnamon, bay leaves, cardamom and cloves and fry until they sizzle.

Add the onions and chillies and fry for 5 minutes, stirring well so they colour evenly. Add the garlic and ginger paste and fry for 1 minute, then add the frozen vegetables and fry for 5 minutes as they defrost and cook out. Add the ground turmeric and salt, stir well and add the cooked rice.

Mix well for 1 minute until the rice is coated with the spices. Turn off the heat and add the garam masala and coriander. Stir well and keep warm. Remove and discard the whole spices before serving.

Gujarati-Style Khichdi with Moong Dal & Vegetables

SERVES 4

100 g (3½ oz/½ cup) *dalia* or cracked wheat

70 g (2¼ oz/scant ½ cup) moong dal, (husked and halved yellow mung beans)

1 litre (34 fl oz/4 cups) water

1 tsp ground turmeric

For the *khichdi*

3 tbsp ghee

1 tsp black mustard seeds

pinch of asafoetida

1 dried red Kashmiri chilli

2.5 cm (1 in) ginger root, finely chopped

8-10 curry leaves

½ tsp Kashmiri chilli powder or mild chilli powder

100 g (3½ oz) carrots, chopped in bite-sized pieces

100 ml (3½ fl oz/scant ½ cup) water

70 g (2¼ oz) tomatoes, chopped

salt, to taste

pinch of sugar

50 g (2 oz) frozen green peas

½ tsp garam masala

chopped coriander (cilantro), to garnish

home-made garlic pickle (page 180), to serve (optional)

Most readers would be familiar with kedgeree, and perhaps even a *khichdi*. This star Gujarati dish takes the flavour up a notch, using moong dal as the base for the *khichdi*. Instead of rice this uses *dalia*, or cracked wheat, which is so nutritious and wholesome. You can add any vegetables you prefer to this versatile dish, including potato, broccoli or green beans.

Put the *dalia*, moong dal, water and ground turmeric in a small saucepan, over a medium heat. Bring to the boil and cook for 20 minutes, stirring every few minutes. Reduce the heat to low and continue cooking for a further 10 minutes. Once cooked, turn off the heat and set aside.

For the *khichdi*, heat the ghee in a large, heavy-based saucepan over a medium heat. Add the mustard seeds, asafoetida and dried chilli, and fry for a few seconds. Add the ginger, curry leaves and chilli powder and fry for 1 minute, then add the carrot and stir well.

Add the water, cover and simmer over a low heat for 5-6 minutes. The carrots will be just cooked. Now add the tomatoes and stir. Season to taste and add the sugar.

Add the cooked *dalia* and moong dal, along with the green peas and stir for 1 minute, still over a low heat until heated through. Add the garam masala. Stir well. Serve warm, garnished with fresh coriander or a drizzle of garlic pickle, if you like.

CONDIMENTS & RAITAS

The recipes here are a mix of pickles and raitas that lend your thali spice, texture and the required sourness (in small amounts!). I am rather proud to be sharing the recipe for *Gajjar Mewa nu Achar* (page 178) – it's been part of our family for over fifty years. I hope you all love it in equal measure.

MAKES ABOUT
1.2 KG (2 LB 6 OZ)

4 tbsp raisins
100 g (3½ oz) dried
   apricots, thinly sliced
150 g (5 oz) soft pitted
   dates, thinly sliced
200 ml (7 fl oz/scant 1 cup)
   white wine vinegar
2 tbsp ghee
650 g (1 lb 7 oz) carrots,
   peeled and coarsely
   grated
350 g (12 oz/scant 2 cups)
   light soft brown sugar
½ tsp garlic powder
½ tsp Kashmiri chilli
   powder or mild chilli
   powder
1 tsp ground nutmeg
1 tsp ground cardamom

PARSI GAJJAR MEWA NU ACHAR

Sticky Carrot, Date & Apricot Chutney

Nothing spells celebration like being part of a Parsi *bhonu* (traditional feast or celebratory occasion), and this sticky, sweet and moreish *achar*, or chutney, is a favourite among Parsis: it's served at every family gathering and occasion.

Put the raisins, apricots and dates in a bowl with half the vinegar and leave to soak for 1–2 hours. (The fruits should have absorbed all the vinegar.)

Heat the ghee in a heavy-based saucepan over a medium heat. Add the grated carrots and sugar and cook for 12 minutes. Add the soaked dried fruit, stir well and continue cooking for 8 minutes.

At this stage, add the garlic powder, chilli powder and nutmeg, then stir well and add the remaining vinegar. Cover and cook over a low heat for 12 minutes, stirring a few times to make sure it doesn't stick to the bottom of the pan.

Add the cardamom and simmer without a lid for 2–3 minutes, then turn the heat off. The *achar* will become sticky and thicken as it cools.

Decant into sterilised jars, seal and store store in the refrigerator. Once opened consume within 2–3 weeks.

Spicy Garlic & Chilli Pickle

**MAKES ABOUT
480 G (1 LB 1 OZ)**

150 ml (5 fl oz/scant ⅔ cup) mustard oil
70 garlic cloves, peeled and trimmed
½ tsp ground turmeric
2 tsp Kashmiri chilli powder or mild chilli powder
½ tsp asafoetida
50 g (2 oz) dark soft brown sugar or jaggery
½ tsp salt
juice of 1 lime

For the spice blend
1 heaped tbsp coriander seeds
1 tbsp black mustard seeds
2 tsp cumin seeds
1 tsp fenugreek seeds

My travels to Jaipur are never complete without visiting family homes and sampling the array of chutneys and pickles served on a thali. On one such visit, I chanced upon this pickle. The spice blend includes Kashmiri chilli powder, which gives the pickle its vibrant colour, while jaggery lends the much-needed sticky sweetness to balance the heat, although here I have used dark brown sugar for convenience. Preparing the garlic is a labour of love, but you can use frozen whole peeled garlic cloves, which are readily available.

Put all the spices into a spice grinder and grind to a fine powder. Set aside.

Heat the oil in a large saucepan over a medium heat. Add the garlic cloves and fry for 2 minutes, then add the turmeric, chilli and asafoetida. Stir well and reduce the heat to low. Add the sugar, salt and spice blend. Fry for 2–3 minutes over a low heat, stirring continuously, then add the lime juice and turn off the heat. Stir well and leave to cool.

Decant into sterilised jars, seal and store store in the refrigerator. Once opened consume within 2–3 weeks.

See recipe photo on page 183

BENGALI TAMATAR CHUTNEY
Tomato Chutney with Nigella Seeds & Chilli

MAKES ABOUT
600 G (1 LB 5 OZ)

5 tbsp vegetable oil
1 heaped tsp fennel seeds
1 tsp cumin seeds
1 tsp nigella seeds
2 dried mild red chillies
800 g (1 lb 12 oz) tomatoes, roughly chopped
1 tsp Kashmiri chilli powder or mild chilli powder
250 g (9 oz) jaggery or soft brown sugar
100 ml (3½ fl oz/scant ½ cup) malt vinegar
pinch of salt

If you want a sweet element that lends itself to a Bengali meal, this tomato chutney is a favourite. An essential part of thalis in east India, it is flavoured with mustard oil, nigella seeds and ginger and cooked until it is rich and syrupy.

Heat the oil in a heavy-based saucepan over a medium heat. Add the whole spices, along with the dried chillies and fry for a few seconds. Add the tomatoes and cook for 10 minutes. As they begin to break down, add the chilli powder, jaggery, vinegar and salt. Stir well and reduce the heat to low, and continue to cook for 1¼ hours, without a lid, stirring often to make sure the chutney doesn't stick to the bottom of the pan. When the chutney thickens and goes dark in colour, turn off the heat.

Leave to cool, then decant into sterilised jars, seal and store store in the refrigerator. Consume within 2 weeks.

See recipe photo on page 182

Clockwise from the top left: Bengali Tomato Chutney (page 181); Rajasthani Lehsun ka Achaar (page 180); Parsi Gajjar Mewa nu Achar (page 178)

**MAKES ABOUT
360 G (12 ¾ OZ)**

2 tsp black mustard seeds
1 tsp fenugreek seeds
200 ml (7 fl oz/scant 1 cup) mustard oil
½ tsp asafoetida
4 tsp Kashmiri chilli powder or mild chilli powder
180 g (6½ oz) fresh turmeric, peeled and sliced in matchsticks
40 g (1½ oz) ginger root, peeled and, sliced in matchsticks
2 tsp salt
juice of 1 lime
pinch of sugar

PUNJABI HALDI ADRAK KA ACHAR

Turmeric & Ginger Pickle

The abundance of fresh turmeric in regions across India is the perfect excuse to make this pickle. A recipe shared by my mother's friend, it's one that I have eaten for years. Even the simplest dal and chawal needs this turmeric and ginger pickle: spicy, tangy and simple to make. I have used mustard oil in this recipe, but you can always use vegetable oil. If using mustard oil, make sure to smoke it over a high heat and cool before warming it again.

Put the mustard seeds and fenugreek seeds in a pestle and mortar and crush to a coarse powder, then set aside.

Heat the oil in a heavy-based saucepan over a medium heat, until it begins to smoke, then turn off the heat. Quickly add the asafoetida, along with the ground spice powder and chilli powder, and stir together, then add the turmeric and ginger matchsticks and stir well for 1 minute.

Add the salt, lime and sugar, mix well and set aside to allow the spices to flavour the *achar*. Leave to cool, decant into sterilised jars, seal and refrigerate. It will keep in the fridge for a few months.

Green Chilli & Peanut Relish

SERVES 4

1 tsp vegetable oil
8-10 green bird's-eye chillies, slit lengthways
6 garlic cloves, roughly chopped
1 tsp cumin seeds
2 tsp roasted peanuts
2 tbsp chopped coriander (cilantro) leaves
crushed sea salt

Ask any Maharashtrian which is the one relish that is an essential part of our thalis and we will undoubtedly give *thecha* the prime spot. The addition of an occasional burst of heat is always welcome while enjoying a thali. *Thecha* is a savoury spiced relish made with roasted green bird's-eye chillies, charred garlic and coriander. Add crushed sea salt to the relish and serve with your thali.

Heat the oil in a non-stick frying pan (skillet) over a medium heat. Add the green chillies and garlic and fry for 3-4 minutes, stirring well, until softened and beginning to brown. Turn off the heat and transfer to a plate lined with paper towels.

Put the cumin seeds in a pestle and mortar and crush to a coarse mixture, then transfer to a serving bowl. Crush the peanuts and add to the bowl. Then add the green chillies, garlic, coriander leaves and salt to the pestle and mortar. Crush to a coarse mixture, then add to the bowl with the cumin seeds and peanuts. Mix well to a rough consistency. Serve sparingly in your thali as an accompaniment.

Cucumber & Coconut Salad

SERVES 4

450 g (1lb) cucumber, peeled
3 tbsp grated fresh coconut
60 g (2 oz) roasted peanuts, coarsely crushed
1 tsp sugar
juice of 1 lime

For the *tadka*
2 tbsp ghee
1 tsp black mustard seeds
5–6 curry leaves
1 green bird's-eye chilli, finely chopped

This cold salad is a taste sensation of sweet, sour and spice that's much needed amidst all the curries in your thali. Fresh diced cucumber, lime, chilli and roasted crushed peanuts all come together to make a cooling, refreshing salad.

Quarter the cucumber lengthways and remove the seeds. Dice the flesh finely and mix in a bowl with the coconut, roasted peanuts and sugar.

To make the *tadka*, heat a frying pan (skillet) over a medium heat. Melt the ghee and add the mustard seeds. When they sputter, add the curry leaves and green chillies. Turn off the heat and allow to cool slightly, then pour this over the cucumber and stir. Add the lime juice, mix well and serve.

ANDHRA CARROT PACHADI

Mango, Mustard & Carrot Chutney

MAKES ABOUT
540 G (1 LB 3 OZ)

4 dried red Kashmiri chillies
1 tbsp black mustard seeds
110 ml (3¾ fl oz/½ cup)
   warm water
450 g (1 lb) carrots, peeled
120 g (4 oz) unripe mango

For the *tadka*
3 tbsp vegetable oil
pinch of asafoetida
½ tsp black mustard seeds
1 tsp fenugreek seeds
1 tbsp sugar
salt, to taste

A spiced carrot chutney hailing from Andhra in southern India. Although the food there is considered to be fiery and hot, this *pachadi*, or fresh pickle, is brimming with flavour and balance, and is cooked with mustard seeds, chilli and tangy mango for a much-needed sour note.

In a bowl, soak the dried chillies and mustard seeds in the warm water for 30 minutes. Dice half of the carrots finely and set aside. Cut the remaining carrots into rough chunks.

Put the chillies, mustard seeds and the soaking liquid into a blender and blend to a paste. Add the mango and rough carrot chunks to this chilli paste and blend to a coarse paste. Set aside.

To make the *tadka*, heat the oil in a heavy-based saucepan over a medium heat. Add the asafoetida, mustard seeds and fenugreek seeds and fry for 2–3 seconds. Reduce the heat to low and add the finely diced carrots.

Cover and cook for 10 minutes over a low heat, stirring halfway through, until the carrots soften slightly. Turn off the heat, and add the blended paste and sugar. Season to taste and stir well. Serve with rice, *idlis* or *dosa*. You can store any leftover chutney in an airtight jar in the fridge for up to 1 week.

Spicy Aubergine Raita

SERVES 4

300 g (10½ oz) aubergines (eggplants), cut into thick round slices
5 tbsp vegetable oil
1 tsp cumin seeds
½ tsp black peppercorns
160 g (5½ oz/⅔ cup) Greek yoghurt, thinned with about 3 tbsp water
pinch of sugar
salt, to taste
½ tsp Kashmiri chilli powder or mild chilli powder
chopped coriander (cilantro), to garnish

Indians use most vegetables in a raita. The cooling effect of dairy or yoghurt-based dishes is an essential part of a thali to balance the meal, while the inclusion of vegetables gives a wonderful texture. Here, roasted aubergines are cooked with cumin, peppercorn and chilli, then mixed with coriander and creamy yoghurt. You can use any vegetable for this dish, including okra, carrots or even potato.

Preheat the oven to 200°C fan (425°F/gas 7). Put the aubergine slices on a lined baking tray (pan). Brush all the slices with the oil and roast in the oven for 30 minutes.

Add the cumin seeds and peppercorns to a pestle and mortar and grind to a coarse powder. Put the yoghurt in a mixing bowl with the sugar and season with salt.

Place the roasted aubergine in a serving bowl and pour over half the yoghurt. Sprinkle the crushed cumin seeds and peppercorns on top, along with the chilli powder.

Pour over the remaining yoghurt and garnish with fresh coriander. Serve alongside your favourite curry.

Gujarati Mint & Mango Chutney

**MAKES ABOUT
450 G (1 LB)**

300 g (10½ oz) unripe
   mango, roughly chopped
80 g (3 oz) mint leaves
1 green bird's-eye chillies
2 tbsp sugar
salt, to taste
2 tbsp ground almonds
70–80 ml (about 3 fl oz/
   5 tbsp) water
½ tsp cumin seeds,
   coarsely crushed

There are so many mint chutney recipes out there, so choosing one to include in the book just meant it had to be something truly special – and this Gujarati recipe is an absolute gem!

Put the mango, mint leaves, green chilli, sugar, salt and ground almonds in a blender. Add the water and blitz to a smooth, fine paste.

Decant into a bowl and add the crushed cumin seeds. Stir well and serve as an accompaniment to your thali – or even spread over sandwiches.

DESSERTS, SWEET THINGS & DRINKS

It's fair to say Indians love sweets, *mithai* and desserts. The regional specialities shared in this chapter are a perfect addition to any thali. Using ingredients like sweet potatoes and lentils to make desserts might seem unusual, but they work so well in these dishes. Finish the meal with my *Gauti Chai*, or cool down with some *Chaas* (both page 204).

Sweet Potato & Cardamom Dumplings in a Sticky Clove Syrup

SERVES 4

250 g (9 oz) orange sweet
  potatoes
100 g (3½ oz) milk powder
3 tbsp plain (all-purpose)
  flour
1 tsp ground cardamom
½ tsp baking powder
vegetable oil, for greasing
  and deep-frying
handful of crushed
  pistachios, to garnish

For the syrup
300 ml (10 fl oz/1¼ cups)
  water
200 g (7 oz) caster
  (superfine) sugar
5 cloves
generous pinch of
  saffron strands

Think Indian *gulab jamun* but made with sweet potato! These deliciously moist dumplings are commonly made in the east of India, where sweet potato and yam are often used in desserts. With flavours of cardamom, clove and saffron, they make a perfect dish for that Friday evening treat, or even to serve at your next dinner for family and friends.

Preheat the oven to 200°C fan (425°F/gas 7). Place the sweet poatoes in a roasting tin (pan) and roast for 35–40 minutes until tender. Leave to cool completely, then scoop out the flesh into a large mixing bowl. Add the milk powder, flour, ground cardamom and baking powder. Mix gently until it comes together to form a slightly sticky dough. Cover and leave to rest in the fridge for around 15 minutes.

Meanwhile, mix all the syrup ingredients togther in a saucepan, and heat over a medium heat. Simmer the syrup for 20 minutes until it thickens, then set aside in a warm place.

Heat the oil for deep-frying in a small saucepan (fill to about a third of the way up the pan). Test the oil is hot enough by dropping a small square of bread into the oil. If it sizzles and browns in 30 seconds, then the oil is ready.

Oil your palms and taking your cooled dumpling/*pantua* mix, gently form 14 small ball shapes – each about half the size of a golf ball. Don't make them any bigger, as they expand when they soak in the sugar syrup.

Fry the dumplings in batches, a few at a time, until golden brown. Set aside on a plate lined with paper towels to drain while you fry the rest. Now soak the dumplings in the sugar syrup for at least 20 minutes.

To serve, spoon the *pantua* from the syrup into serving bowls and serve warm with extra syrup drizzled generously over. If you like, you can top them with a sprinkling of crushed pistachios. These are equally delcious served cold.

Stewed Apricots with Almonds, Pistachio & Saffron

SERVES 4

300 g (10½ oz) dried apricots
400 ml (13 fl oz/generous 1½ cups) water
20 g (¾ oz) caster (superfine) sugar
generous pinch of saffron
crushed almonds, to garnish
crushed pistachios, to garnish
clotted cream, to serve (optional)

A Hyderabadi special made with stewed apricots, saffron and cream, this is perfect to eat warm just as it is, although even more delicious topped with some clotted cream.

Put the apricots, water and sugar in a saucepan over a medium heat. Cook for 40 minutes until the apricots begin to soften. Stir well, making sure the apricots don't stick to the bottom of the pan.

Add a small amount of the saffron and simmer for a further 5 minutes. Cool the *khubani* and blend to a coarse mix with a stick blender. Add an additional 100 ml (3½ fl oz/scant ½ cup) water and a little more saffron.

Serve warm, topped with almonds and pistachios, along with some clotted cream, if you wish.

PARUPPU PAYASAM

Sweet Moong Dal & Cashew Pudding with Cardamom & Jaggery

SERVES 4

2 tbsp butter or ghee
1 tbsp vegetable oil
6 cloves
200 g (7 oz) moong dal,
   (husked and halved
   yellow mung beans)
800 ml (27 fl oz/3½ cups)
   warm water
200 g (7 oz) jaggery or dark
   soft brown sugar
8 cardamom pods, seeds
 only, ground to a powder
6 cashew nuts, roughly
   broken
150 ml (5 fl oz/scant ⅔ cup)
   coconut milk

This is one Indian dessert that I absolutely love! And I'm sure most south Indians would agree with me. Using lentils in desserts has always been common across India. This *payasam* can also be cooked with coconut oil instead of using butter and vegetable oil.

Heat the butter and oil in a heavy-based saucepan over a low heat. Add the cloves and fry for a few seconds, then add the moong dal and fry, stirring well, for 8–9 minutes. The colour will deepen as it fries. Slowly add the water, making sure it doesn't sputter. Increase the heat slightly, bring the mix to the boil, then cover, and simmer over a low heat for 50 minutes, stirring well a few times during cooking.

While the moong dal is cooking, in a separate saucepan dissolve the jaggery or sugar with 300 ml (10 fl oz/1¼ cups) water and simmer gently for 10–15 minutes. Set aside to cool slightly.

Take the lid off the moong dal and mash to thicken the mixture slightly. Cook for a further 5 minutes, stirring well to make sure it doesn't stick to the bottom of the pan.

Add the jaggery water to the moong dal, along with the ground cardamom and cashew nuts. Stir well and simmer without the lid for 10 minutes. Add the coconut milk and simmer for a further 2–3 minutes. Turn off the heat and serve in bowls, warm or cold. The *payasam* will thicken as it cools.

Deep-Fried Pastry with Coconut, Cardamom, & Jaggery

SERVES 4

For the pastry dough
170 g (6 oz) plain (all-purpose) flour or *maida*, plus extra for dusting and rolling
2 tbsp melted butter or ghee
pinch of salt
90 ml (3 fl oz/⅓ cup) water
2 tsp milk, to seal the *gujiya* pastry

For the coconut stuffing
120 g (4 oz) grated fresh or frozen coconut
80 g (3 oz) jaggery or dark soft brown sugar
¼ tsp ground cardamom
1 tsp raisins
1 tsp white poppy seeds
vegetable oil for deep-frying

Perfect served with chai, this little sweet pastry has been a staple at my home in Mumbai for as long as I can remember. It is also served during festivals and when we had friends over.

To make the stuffing, heat a medium frying pan (skillet) over a low heat. Add the coconut, jaggery and cardamom and fry for 8 minutes. Now add the raisins and poppy seeds and mix well, frying for a further 2 minutes. Turn off the heat and allow the mixture to cool slightly while you make the dough.

Put the flour, melted butter and salt in a large bowl. Mix in the water, a little at a time, to form a smooth dough. Dust with a little flour and knead for 1 minute. Cover and leave to rest for 10 minutes.

Now divide the dough into 14 equal portions. Flatten each piece of dough and roll out on a lightly floured surface to a 4 cm (1½ in) disc. Use a little flour for dusting if it sticks too much. Take one of the pastry discs and add 1 tablespoon of the stuffing to the centre. Brush the edges of the pastry with milk and fold over into a a semi-circle. Press lightly, seal well, and using a fork, crimp the edges (see photographic steps oveleaf). Place the *gujiyas* on a plate and cover with a damp cloth while you make the remaining *gujiyas*.

Fill a saucepan or wok with oil for deep-frying, about a third of the way up, and heat over a medium heat. Once the oil is hot, fry 2 *gujiyas* at a time, turning them while frying, until they are golden brown. They will puff up slightly and have a crisp coating. Set aside on a plate lined with paper towels and keep warm while you fry the remainder.

As an alternative, you can bake the *gujiyas* if you prefer. Preheat the oven to 200°C fan (425°F/gas 7). Make all the *gujiyas* and place on a lined baking tray. Brush with butter or ghee. Bake for around 15–17 minutes until crisp and light brown all over.

These are best served warm or at room temperature. Store in an airtight container and eat within a few days.

See recipe photo overleaf

DESSERTS, SWEET THINGS & DRINKS

GAUTI CHAI
Chai Infused with Cardamom & Lemongrass

SERVES 4

500 ml (17 fl oz/2 cups) whole milk
150 ml (5 fl oz/scant ⅔ cup) water
8 green cardamom pods, seeds only
6 cm (2½ in) cinnamon stick
2 lemongrass stalks, trimmed and roughly chopped
3 strong tea bags
3 tsp sugar

Unlike most masala chai recipes, this one does not have a long list of ingredients! But it does include one of my favourite ingredients – lemongrass. It is a lovely chai recipe – refreshing and simple to rustle up.

Place the milk and water in a saucepan over a medium heat. Bring to the boil, then reduce the heat to low and add the remaining ingredients.

Simmer over a low heat for 15–17 minutes, stirring often to make sure it does not stick to the bottom of the pan or boil over. Strain into mugs and drink warm.

MATTHA/CHAAS
Cooling Yoghurt Drink

SERVES 4

320 g (10¾ oz/1⅓ cups) Greek yoghurt
400 ml (13 fl oz/generous 1½ cups) water
generous amount of salt, to taste
1 tsp cumin seeds
1 green bird's-eye chilli, deseeded
2.5 cm (1 in) ginger, roughly chopped
1 tbsp finely chopped coriander (cilantro)

The perfect thirst-quencher, this is also a great way to stay hydrated after a thali.

Put the yoghurt, water and salt in a jug and whisk well until smooth. Put the cumin, chilli and ginger in a pestle and mortar and crush to a coarse mix.

Add this to the yoghurt mix, along with the fresh coriander, and stir well. Serve chilled.

REGIONAL THALIS

The landscape of India is as diverse as the regions that make up this vibrant nation. With thalis eaten across the country, I want to share a glimpse of four regional communities with menus that celebrate some of the recipes in this book. I hope this will give you an insight into the food included in different regional thalis, and some ideas that you can try at home.

GUJARATI THALI

A visual feast of colours, textures and flavours, this thali is packed with Gujarati classics. The key to thalis from this region is how they balance the sweet as well as savoury elements within one meal. Including pulses, lentils and seasonal vegetables, this thali reflects how varied the region is when it comes to recipes, with dishes hailing from Ahmedabad, Surat and Kathiawad.

Gujarati Surati Dal (page 146)

Gujarati Vaghara Makkai (page 42)

Gujarati Rangoon na Vaal (page 118)

Fada ni Khichdi (page 174)

Ringan Batata nu Shaak (page 105)

Coconut Gujiya (page 201)

Khamang Kakdi (page 187)

Gujarati Moong Dal Dhokla (page 152)

Hari Pudine ki Chutney (page 192)

Phulka (page 164)

ANDHRA THALI

If there is one region I urge you to explore while planning your travels across the southern coast of India, it is Andhra Pradesh. One of my first visits there dispelled every myth I had heard about the cuisine! I experienced what I can only describe as a heady mix of regional influences: the array of vegetables, spices, pickles, chutneys and crispy fried snacks is endless. There are influences from the southern coast, including curry leaves, coconut and tamarind, along with a liberal use of ground spices, that sit comfortably alongside Hyderabadi and Nizam cuisine, bringing you their rich heritage of street food, including kebabs, biryanis and salans.

Andhra Kodi Vepudu (page 54)

Andhra Vankaya Pulusu (page 88)

Andhra Muthapappu (page 117)

Andhra Masala Vadai (page 155)

Andhra Tomato Paappu (page 142)

Andhra Carrot Pachadi (page 188)

Paruppu Payasam (page 200)

Tamarind Rice (page 170)

Roti

BENGALI THALI

Bengalis love their food, which is built around traditional recipes and the elaborate use of spices and local ingredients. But beyond that, sharing these meals with family and friends is what, for me, sums up the warmth and joy of a Bengali feast: enjoying delicious food while discussing literature and current affairs. From steamed rice served with ghee, cholar dal, stir-fried vegetables and chutneys to mustard-laden fish curries and aromatic meat dishes, the flavours are subtle, and the cooking style classic.

Bengali Tomato Chutney (page 181)

Bengali Begun Pora (page 35)

Bengali Cholar Dal (page 138)

Bengali Pantua (page 196)

Bengali Beetroot Chop (page 160)

Puris (page 167)

Bengali Khosha Charchari (page 43)

Kumro Chenchki (page 108)

Bengali Kancha Lonka Murgi (page 50)

Plain Rice

PUNJABI THALI

The land of five rivers (*panj* meaning 'five' and *ab* meaning 'water' in the Persian language) is brimming with vibrance and unapologetic flavours. This thali is packed with robust flavour and celebrates an array of cooking techniques. Punjabi cuisine includes slow-cooked meat curries, fresh vegetables and dairy. Paneer, yogurt and milk are all locally produced, along with a variety of grains including wheat, millet and maize, which are grown across the region.

Tariwala Murgh (page 52)

Chutney Wale Aloo (page 102)

Punjabi Matar Paneer (page 110)

Khumb Matar Malai (page 92)

Tadka Dal (page 145)

Vegetable Pulao (page 173)

Ajwain Paratha (page 168)

Baingan Raita (page 191)

Punjabi Haldi Adrak ka Achar (page 185)

Shakkarkand ki Tikki (page 156)

MENU PLANNING

Here I have put together some recipe selections for you to serve a vegan, vegetarian, fish, everyday or celebration thali.

Vegan Thali

Use vegetable oil or coconut oil in recipes if alternatives are required

Andhra Carrot Pachadi (page 188)
Malabar Mezhukupuratti (page 39)
Gujarati Vaghara Makkai (page 42)
Bedmi Aloo (page 90)
Punjabi Rajma Masala (page 114)
Rajasthani Palak Dal (page 143)
Kothimbir Vade (page 150)
Phulka (page 164)
Paruppu Payasam (page 200)
plain rice

Vegetarian Thali

Bengali Tomato Chutney (page 181)
Punjabi Kadhai Paneer (page 30)
Khumb Mattar Malai (page 92)
Goan Dalicha Ras (page 140)
Punjabi Khatte Chole (page 91)
Andhra Masala Vadai (page 155)
Phulka (page 164)
Vegetable Pulao (page 173)
plain yoghurt and fresh fruit

Fish Thali

Khamang Kakdi (page 187)
Rahjasthani Lehsun ka Achar (page 180)
Kerala Fish Moilee (page 122)
Bangda Masala (page 125)
Goan Prawn Balchao (page 134
Andhra Tomato Paappu (page 142)
Tamarind Rice (page 170)
Phulka (page 164)
Khubani ka Meetha (page 198)

Everyday Thali

Maharashtrian Batatachi Bhaaji (page 36)
Rajasthani Achari Kaddu ki Sabzi (page 33)
Tadka Dal (page 145)
Phulka (page 164)
Punjabi Haldi Adrak ka Achar (page 185)
plain rice and yoghurt

Celebration Thali

Parsi Gajjar Mewa nu Achar (page 178)
Hari Pudine ki Chutney (page 192)
Rajasthani Gobi Rajwadi (page 41)
Bengali Kancha Lonka Murgi (page 50)
Gavraan Muttonacha Rassa (page 83)
Punjabi Matar Paneer (page 110)
Bengali Cholar Dal (page 138)
Shakkarkand ki Tikki (page 156)
Ajwain Paratha (page 168)
Vegetable Pulao (page 173)
Bengali Pantua (page 196)

ACKNOWLEDGEMENTS

They say it takes a village! And I feel lucky to be surrounded by an incredible group of people who have been my anchor, raised me up and supported the work I do.

Bharat – So grateful for this life with you. You truly are the calm to my chaos. There aren't words to say how proud I am of us, the life we share and how you define 'husband goals'. For your incredible spirit, thoughtful and supportive words and creating many more memories, lots of laughs and adventures ahead.

Johann – My kind hearted and joyful one! Thank you always for being my fiercest supporter and always giving mum a thumbs up for the meals she cooks. For seeing the bright side in every situation and growing up to be the most wonderful human being. I am so immensely proud of you.

Kajal – It has been a privilege to have had the opportunity to work with you. For you, to lead this book with wisdom, patience and encouragement. *Thali* is as much yours as it is mine and I couldn't have asked for a better editor to work with.

Holly –Thank you for your belief, instinct and always being the sounding board a girl needs that's just phone call away. For being the creative force with a kind heart thats steering me in the right direction.

Sam – Your images bring each and every recipe to life. A keen eye, sensibility for the dish and making the time to find out about the stories behind these recipes. I am thrilled to have you part of this book and to see how stunning it looks. And **Matt** for being so lovely and always at the ready with a cuppa!

Val – To see you cook my recipes exactly as I imagined they would be, was such a thrill. Thank you for your kind words through it all, its has truly meant the world. You are the best. And **Hannah** for keeping us all going and for being an absolute star.

Alex – For the most wonderful props and keeping the aesthetics of Indian cooking alive through the pages. Such a joy to have worked with you.

Daniel – Thank you for putting together the design for Thali. Filling it with joy, colour and soul.

To my amazing friends who have seen me through the last year while I wrote, tested and cooked all the recipes. For letting me feed you all copious curries, and in return always sending me heaps of praise but more than anything offering your kind words, its meant more than you know – Helen, Mythilli, Sarah, Sean, Brooke, Paul, Rachel, Bridget, Pooja, Samyukta, Petra, Jo, Arpita, Maurice and Hannah.

Lastly I want to thank you – my amazing readers, followers and those who have read and cooked my recipes. You have no idea how surreal it still is, knowing that recipes I write at my desk make their way into your home kitchens and fill your dinner tables with joy. Thank you, thank you always x

ABOUT THE AUTHOR

Growing up in India, food was an intrinsic part of family life for Maunika, with secret recipes and traditions passed down from generations. Following on from her internationally loved debut cookbook, *Indian Kitchen*, Maunika has amassed a global following of cooks who have fallen in love with her cooking style and traditional Indian recipes that are accessible and achievable that you'll want to cook time & time again.

Maunika's work has seen her travel to countries including America, Spain and Norway as well as continuing to explore her native India. She's a popular contributor to titles including *Good Housekeeping*, *BBC Food* and *Olive Magazine*, and is the contributing editor for *Vogue India* often writing about the London food scene.

INDEX

Published in 2021 by Hardie Grant Books,
an imprint of Hardie Grant Publishing

Hardie Grant Books (London)
5th & 6th Floors
52–54 Southwark Street
London SE1 1UN

Hardie Grant Books (Melbourne)
Building 1, 658 Church Street
Richmond, Victoria 3121

hardiegrantbooks.com

British Library Cataloguing-in-Publication Data. A catalogue record for this book
is available from the British Library.

Thali
ISBN: 978-1-78488-458-1

10 9 8 7 6 5 4 3 2

Publisher: Kajal Mistry
Design and Artwork: Daniel New
Photographer: Sam A. Harris
Home Economist and Food Stylist: Valerie Berry
Prop Stylist: Alexander Breeze
Copy-editor: Wendy Hobson
Proofreader: Tara O'Sullivan
Indexer: Vanessa Bird
Production Controller: Nikolaus Ginelli

Colour reproduction by p2d
Printed and bound in China by Leo Paper Products Ltd.

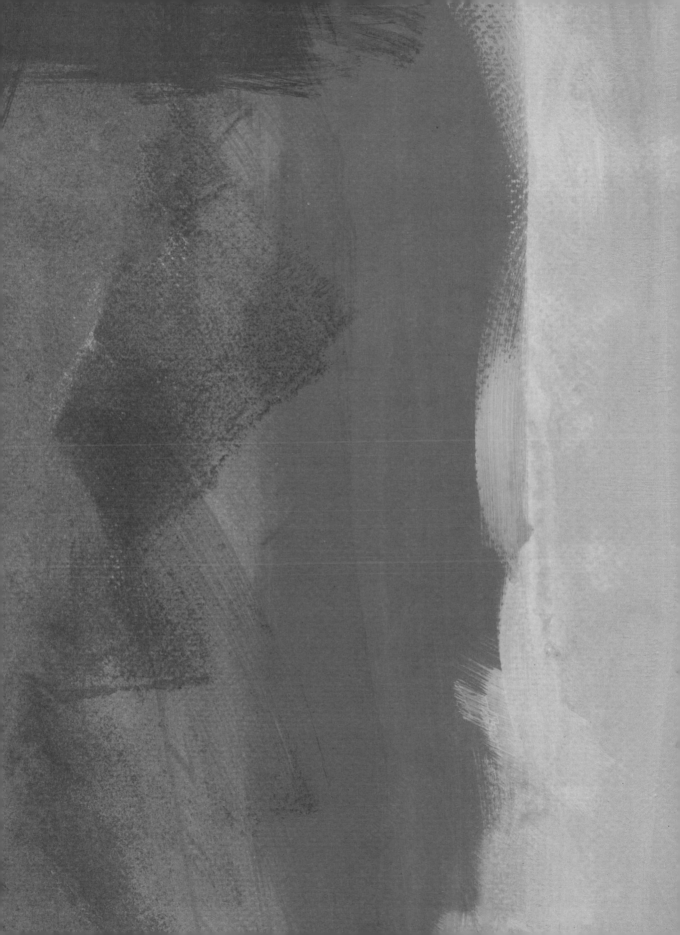